NO MATTER

A DRAMA ON THE INFERENCE OF DESIGN

VANCE CARTRIGHT

Prologue

This book is based on two valid premises: That the universe had a beginning, (that is that at one time it did not exist and then it exploded into existence), and that anything that begins to exist has a cause. The universe has certain rules, also known as universal constants, which control the manner in which it exists and operates. Almost all scientists agree that the universal constants, for example one of them is gravity, are set so precisely that it cannot be possible that they occurred by chance. Intelligent design advocates claim that the settings as they are, compared to what they could be, are indicative of a planned design which allows life as we know it to exist. In rebuttal to that concept those scientists who disagree claim that there is another possibility, which is that if enough other universes continually popped into existence along with our universe, each with different settings, inevitably our universe with all its settings which permits life, would occur by chance. The odds for multi universes to produce the settings of our universe are enormous, something like flipping a coin a trillion times in a row and having the coin come up heads every time, but given enough time, according to those scientists, it could happen.

So there are theoretically only two possible explanations for existing conditions which allow life on our planet, design or chance. In this novel this theoretical debate is explored in a proposed real life situation in the hope that a common sense dramatic presentation, (rather than a boring debate filled with philosophical and unbelievably technical argument), would make the issues more understandable. Don't be discouraged by the facts that are presented here, the scientists have done the work to prove the facts, all you have to do is use common sense to decide which version makes the most sense to you.

Chapter One

John Taylor was sitting in his office with his head propped up by his hands, his elbows resting on his knees. His office door was partially closed and he told his secretary, Pam Foster, to hold all his calls. Pam knew why. John was suffering while trying to figure out what he had done wrong in a trial he had just finished and lost. He had represented a man who fell through a roof, thirty feet to a concrete floor. The man, Roger Gibbs, could no longer walk and suffered from a closed head injury which changed his entire personality. It was affecting his relationship with his wife. He needed medical help and he needed money to get it. He should have won his case, the contractor he worked for was negligent. But he lost, and John Taylor felt it was his fault. He was suffering, he just sat there repeating "Oh God, Oh God."

Frank Warner entered John's office. He knew John would be hurting. He and John were in the same class in law school. After graduation Frank had specialized in criminal defense while John handled civil litigation. They had remained good friends. Frank entered and spoke to Pam,

"Here's the best friend and companion attorney to bring balm to heal the wounds. Is the patient taking a little nourishment yet?"

Pan replied,

"He's not there yet."

Frank looks into the office, sees John and comments to Pam,

"This is going to take more than two aspirins and a night's rest." John hears him and says,

"I'm a total failure."

Frank had planned in advance what he would say. Being a lawyer he relied on logic. It was not a good choice to heal the spirit.

"Look John, this isn't the first time a lawyer lost a case. Remember Sam DuPont in Kansas City turned down ten million on that ground water pollution case and lost?"

John brushed the example aside. He lifted his head and looked at Frank.

"He trusted me Frank. He hired me to use professional judgment and I let him down. I let him turn down a half a million settlement offer."

John stood up and looked out the window behind his desk.

"I don't think I'm capable of professional judgment which means I shouldn't be in this business. I've set up my life along a plan that I can't fulfill. All those years in college and law school for a plan than failed."

"John you're over reacting. You've been one of the most successful trial attorneys in this Midwestern area and you've run a successful law office for eight years. You've helped a lot of people."

Frank tried more logic.

"As far as the Gibbs case is concerned the worker's comp insurer had paid $400,000 in medical expense and would have been entitled to re-imbursement for that amount which meant that Gibbs would have gotten practically nothing if he settled for that amount. It was a reasonable decision for him to turn down the settlement and take a chance on trial."

"Yeah sure, it was a reasonable business to turn down a half a million dollar settlement."

"I'm speaking the truth John. He would have ended up with next to nothing after the worker's comp insurer got its cut. He didn't lose much by rolling the dice. When it comes down to it you are the one who lost by putting all the time and effort into the case and since you took the case on a contingent basis you got nothing, and John I watched the trial; you put together a great trial. Everybody thought you had a sure winner."

Seeing his logic was having little or no affect Frank, knowing his friend well, went to what he really thought was the heart of the matter. He drew in his breath and boldly said,

"But John, as your friend I want to ask you, are you really mourning the loss for Gibbs or are you mourning the loss of the prestige you suffered by not getting a big verdict? Let's face it Buddy that's a big kick in the teeth but one that a lawyer's got to be able to take, shrug it off and go on with his business."

Frank looked intently at his friend as he asked that question. He saw John look startled, then a trace of anger made a fleeting appearance on his face but quickly changed to a thoughtful expression. John began to realize that perhaps his old buddy had hit the nail on the head but he didn't want to address that directly yet.

"I suppose your argument is logical. You're thinking like a lawyer but it's hard to be logical when this poor man suffered a loss."

John heard himself make the reply to Frank's logical argument and thought to himself that it sounded lame. He paused, then looked Frank in the eye and said,

"I have to admit that I thought I had a case that would result in the first million dollar verdict in this county. That was an ego trip. And I guess that could be a big part of my feeling of guilt." He paused:

"I guess I needed that Frank. I'm glad you're around to give good advice when it's needed. Now I realize why I feel so bad. I'll have to take it as a lesson learned. But it still hurts."

"We all know what it feels like to lose a case but it is part of the business. That's what buddies are for Johnny, and all that for my standard fee. Now, having done my deed, I have to run."

"It's still going to be hard to show my face around the court house, everyone knows what happened."

Ignoring John's comment, Frank looks at Pam,

"Pam, I think you better get this man back to work, he's got clients to represent".

Frank waves goodbye and leaves while Pam comments that John has the Sanborn living trust to execute and the Conway trial is in two weeks. John, getting back to business, asks Pam to get him the Conway case and set up an appointment for Danny Conway and his father to come in. John is back at his desk as Pam brings him the Conway file. John opens the file and reads it and then thinks to himself,

"Danny, how did you ever get yourself in this mess?"

John is six foot one inch tall and is slender but muscular with a wide chest and shoulders. He has black strait hair that tends to fall down on his forehead. With high cheekbones and a straight nose he presents a handsome face but it is the way his upper lip seems to fall into a constant smile that makes him attractive and likeable.

Pam leaves work at 4:30 and John is still working on various matters when Danny Conway knocks softly on his office door.

"Danny, I wasn't expecting you until Friday."

"Mr. Taylor, I'd like to talk to you alone without my father here."

"Sure Danny, sit down."

Danny sits in front of John's desk with his head down and shoulders slumped.

"Mr. Taylor, I've got to talk to someone. I can't talk to my dad."

"I'm your lawyer, Danny. Everything you say to me is confidential. Nobody else hears it. Not even your dad."

"It's just that I can't do anything to please him. Everything I try to do, I don't succeed. My dad is such a manly guy. He was the quarter back on our high school football team when they won the State class C championship. He was drafted and was in combat in Vietnam. He's the plant supervisor at Mr. Stryker's factory. He's so sure of himself. He expects the same from me. Mr. Taylor, I try as hard as I can. He wanted me to be the quarterback on the team. I don't have the arm for it. The best I could do was make the second string wide receiver. Last season I only caught one pass in a game. Now in my senior year I'm not the go to guy for our quarterback."

"Danny you're in high school. How many touchdowns you score isn't going to mean one thing in whatever career you choose. You've got a long life ahead of you and Danny in preparing your case I talked to your teacher, Mr. Sylvester, about you and he tells me you're an excellent student. And you're in the 99th percentile. Believe me Danny you'll excel in whatever you do."

"Do you really think so Mr. Taylor?"

"I'm absolutely positive about it Danny."

"Mr. Sylvester is my favorite teacher. We have long talks sometimes. I can talk to him about science and physics and the universe, I think cosmology is really interesting. I tried to talk to my father about cosmology and he said 'No child of mine is going to be a beauty operator'."

"You're a good and valuable person Danny. Now let me finish preparing your case so we can get you out of this mess."

"Yes sir, bye Mr. Taylor, I appreciate your advice."

John scribbled a few notes and closes his file for the evening. As he leaves and locks the office Danny is still on his mind. He says as if he were talking to Danny,

"Danny, you're putting too much importance on the wrong thing."

Little did he realize it was a fault he had in common with Danny.

Chapter Two

John went straight home to his apartment, showered and got dressed for a party that Greg Stryker was holding at his home. The party was for some of the purchasers who ordered the parts that Stryker Industrial manufactured for automobiles and various appliances. Drinks were being served and conversations were going full force as Greg maneuvered from one couple to another. John was invited because Stryker's daughter, Jill, was engaged to be married to John. Many thought it was a match made in heaven. Jill thought John was a good catch as a thirty-four year old bachelor who could be very successful if he'd accept the contacts her father could create for him. But if it were a match made in heaven there was trouble in paradise since John completely rejected her father's help in building his career and insisted he establish himself as at least one of the best and successful trial lawyers in the tri-county area. He could not let himself become what he considered a lackey relying on his father-in-law for recognition. This was one reason he would take extra time with a client even if it would make him late for one of Jill's social occasions. It made him feel independent.

As Greg Stryker made small talk with his clients Jill was sitting with a fellow socialite, Linda Coleman, in a corner settee and cocktail table. Linda spoke,

"I smell food cooking Jill, any chance your fiancé will arrive before we're seated or is he going to pop up out of a cake"?

"It's inexcusable Linda. All he thinks about is work. He doesn't give a thought about how embarrassing it is for me to be delaying a wedding date. Mother doesn't know what to do. He's set his mind on being successful as a lawyer in that silly business of his. I went to his office a few days ago and all he could talk about was losing that case. I wanted to have a serious conversation about a wedding date but he was so down about that case he didn't pay any attention to me."

Linda responded in a slightly sarcastic manner,

"Oh, then you weren't able to cheer him up."

"Linda, my mission was to set a date. He'll be fine. Besides if he'd just forget about that business of his and let dad back him for district attorney he'd be established in a prestige job. Instead he envisions himself as a great trial attorney dominating the court room, getting great respect when in fact some in our circle of friends are calling him a bump and bruise attorney".

"I wouldn't let him hear you call him that. He'll go into another lecture about the noble lawyer defending the downtrodden and Jill, he really believes that. Oh, here he is now."

John comes into the room and makes his way over to Jill and Linda.

"Sorry I'm late, I got tied up with a client and couldn't get away."

"That's right John. Put your clients above all else."

Linda, trying to avoid any stress between the two comments,

"I think they're calling us to dinner."

"Jill, when you're representing a client you have part of their life in your hands. It takes up part of your life, you can't just shut them off. Helping them out is part of being a human being."

Linda tries again,

"Isn't it warm for this time of year?" Jill, ignoring her, continues,

"I'm part of your life too but you don't seem to take that into consideration."

The dinner bell rings softly. Linda interjects with relief,

"Well… no need to make the obvious comment."

John, smiling, says,

"Let's take some nourishment between rounds."

At the dinner table John is smiling as Jill puts on a pleasant face which doesn't represent her current mood. She was five foot four with a round face and wore her hair in a page boy to hide it. Her blonde hair was betrayed by its roots. Her serious nature, known to all, made it difficult to hide her true feelings.

Soon the adult beverages relax tensions and the roast beef dinner satisfied all. Greg Stryker called for cognac as an after dinner drink. It was a pleasant evening and as the party began to recede, Steve Sylvester, Danny's teacher, sought out John and pulled him aside.

"John, I wanted to have a word with you about Dan Conway. I know he's very worried about these charges. I hope you can help him. He told me about how he was stopped for speeding and the police found a marijuana cigarette in his coat pocket. He was at a party with the football team and he was offered a marijuana cigarette which he took because the others were using them and he didn't want to look like he wasn't one of them. He put it out right away and put it in his pocket and forget about it until he was stopped by the police."

"John, he's very bright and sensitive. He's one of the top students in the school but he doesn't have confidence in himself. He pushes himself to be an outstanding football player like his father was but his talent isn't in athletics, it's in his brain. He's judging himself by someone else's standard. It's a shame."

John commented,

"He told me he enjoys science. He says you two talk about cosmology the earth, the stars, the universe." Steve replies,

"I wanted to talk to you about something else also. It's my job at Roosevelt High. I try to think like a true scientist. I want to consider facts in an unbiased manner and question established norms. You may think I'm somewhat of a purist but, for example, I teach both sides of the global warming issue because there are respected scientists who disagree with the computer theory it's based on and I teach evidence of design of the universe because there are some respected cosmologists and microbiologists who find significant evidence of design."

"I can understand you following your intellect on something like that. Why do you bring it up, is there a problem?"

"Yes, some of the members of the school board object and say I'm leading the students astray from what they consider settled science and injecting religion into their lives. John there's no such thing as settled science. At one time a flat earth was settled science. Bloodletting was so called settled science. If you close your mind to different concepts then you've closed out the richness and discovery of true science".

"Has there been any action taken against you by the school board?"

"Yes and that's why I bring it up. There's a hearing set up at the end of this month. I don't know what they plan to do but I'm not going to let them affect the way I teach. I'm not going to be an instrument to close the minds of these young people."

"I don't see this as a big issue in the community. People don't know about this and there's not going to be any pressure on the board to act one way or the other. I say let them have their hearing. You explain your position and the whole thing will go away."

"I hope you're right John."

"If there is any further action let me know and I'll see what I can do to help"

"Thanks John, I'll be in touch. Good night."

"Good night."

Chapter Three

The next day, a Saturday, John is at his desk, working. Gregg Stryker enters the office, walks silently to John's office and knocks.

"Gregg, come in".

"Hello John, I thought you'd be working on a Saturday. I need men like you at my plant....John, I hope I didn't give you the wrong impression the last time we talked. I could see that you were upset but you know I'm a hard business man and when I set my mind to do something I do whatever is necessary to accomplish it."

"I know Gregg but the law business is a different matter. Things have to be done ethically or else everything that the law stands for, fairness and justice, are meaningless. And by no stretch of the imagination was your offer to get people on the jury who would rule in my favor ethical or fair".

"Fair play and honesty are great sounding words but if you know the way deals that are made for judicial appointments, for seats on the city council, how money and back scratching plays a part in those positions, you'd see that playing the game by your own rules is necessary to succeed. That's how I made it in my business and John you see the results. I've got the largest factory in town and growing and I employ 700 people at the plant which I think most people in town would consider a good thing. I'm a fighter John and the way I do things is no different than the way people are doing things to me. It's the way things are done."

"Maybe so Gregg but I don't think the law is that type of business. I know you believe that decisions are made in back room deals but I believe that the law is based on logic and common sense and lifetime experiences. It's written and decided by honest men trying their best to achieve a noble goal. That's why I went into the legal field and perhaps lately I've neglected that goal but I can see that that's the ideal and I'm not going to give up on it now."

"Well I can't fault you for that. As a matter of fact that's why I think you'd make a good district attorney and the committee is about to decide whom to back. The time is right John. Be a successful prosecutor and the door can be opened to judgeships, even the Supreme Court. You'll be established and ready to settle down, marry and start a family, which I assume is a significant part of your goal as well. Otherwise you wouldn't have asked Jill to marry you."

John seems somewhat startled when Gregg mentions marriage sensing that Gregg's mission is to get him to set a wedding date.

"It's not that I'm unappreciative Gregg but dealing with criminal law alone as a prosecutor is restricting and becomes routine. I enjoy the full exposure of issues that arise in the lives of people. Variety appeals to me. It keeps me on my toes. I know that settling down and setting a wedding date is appealing to some but it's not right for me at this time."

Greg, believing that John thinks his true purpose was to get him to set a wedding date, feigns indignity "If you think I came here just to get you to set a wedding date..."

John interrupts: "No Gregg, I know you would not come here for that reason (slight pause) alone. You don't operate that way. You came because we had that disagreement about the jury issue and I appreciate that we've had this chance to understand each other. Shake?"

Gregg, shaking his hand, says,

"Good John. In my business dealings I like to look a person in the eye and know where we stand. Good to talk to you John and the offer is still open if you should change your mind."

"Thanks Gregg I feel the same way and I thank you for coming." John walks him to the door.

"Good bye John".

"Good bye sir." Gregg leaves. John watches him go and says out of Gregg's hearing, "Yes sir. I very much appreciate the opportunity to understand the way you think".

Chapter Four

A week passes, it is Friday afternoon. Frank, the criminal defense lawyer and Sam Frink are at the Bench and Bar, a saloon close to the court house which is the favorite of the trial lawyers. A sign at the bar proclaims, *"Best hamburgers in the Midwest"* People are seated at tables. Frank and Sam, who is an assistant prosecutor, are standing at the bar. Katy Newton and Pam are also present at a table chatting quietly. Frank and Sam are talking about the criminal trial they just finished in which Frank's client was convicted and Sam was victorious. Others are in the bar talking quietly and Frank and Sam are laughing and joking. Frank speaks.

"Well, let it be known that in the case of People v. Carl Hunt that Sam the prosecutor man was victorious".

"Even I didn't think the jury would come in that fast. You did a good job of raising doubt about whether it was really your client who was shown on the surveillance tape robbing the store. We didn't have much evidence other than the surveillance tape and it was hard to identify your client. It could have been anyone."

"Yeah, I was sure I raised a question in the minds of jurors about him not being the robber and I felt I had a sure acquittal even after you showed the tape and no one could identify the person on the tape unless they knew the man very well. But Sam I never dreamed my client, when he saw the tape, would jump up and say (Frank says this loudly in a voice imitating his client),

'Hey, that's me there'."

Both laugh. "Well that was enough for the jury to convict, but take heart Frank, you've beaten me enough that I had to win sometime."

As they turn back to the bar and tip their drinks Pam and a Katy are sitting at the table talking as they eat their meal. Katy, Frank's secretary says,

"Look at Frank. I typed a brief for him that he worked his heart out on and then the client blows the case. I know it was like a punch in the stomach to him but there he is laughing it up with the prosecutor who just beat him. I can't get over how these guys can fight like cats and dogs in the court room and come out and be pals when it's over".

"They've got to Katy. If they kept it inside themselves they'd never last as trial lawyers. Coming to the Bench and Bar watering hole is part of the re-entry process into the normal world. Look at us, we even need to settle down. We set their appointments and depositions. We type their briefs. Every things a rush with last minute changes and motions to be typed after court closes at 4:00 which must be ready when the case continues the next morning. It's taxing, it's crazy, and it's exciting working with someone who's dedicated to their job."

"You're right. It keeps us on our toes. And it sounds as though you have an admiration for a certain good looking bachelor who fits bill in every respect expect not being available." Pam says,

"Of course as his secretary I'm interested in what he does. But I'm not the type of girl who would interfere in the relationship with his fiancé. And don't you ever think he'd ever marry just for money. He won't marry until he becomes what he considers a success entirely on his own so he isn't beholding to her family."

"Ok girl. I believe everything you say but watch that admiration thing. It can grow into something that could be a big hurt. Oh, oh, look who just walked in."

John comes into the bar, sees and waves to Frank and Sam, then sees Pam and Katy and goes to their table.

"I'm going to get a bite to eat, mind if I join you?"

Katy looks at Pam to see how she reacts. Pam says, "Not at all". Then Katy responds,

"Not at all but I was just leaving. The big game is tonight and it already must be half over."

"I didn't know you were a football fan Katy.'

"I'm usually not John but my nephew's on our team and if we win tonight we'll go on to a class C championship game so it's a big thing for the town. It's even being broadcasted on the local radio station and I've got to get there before the game is over. I bet it's already in the fourth quarter", She says as she leaves.

John sits down, they smile at each other. The waitress comes to the table and asks John.

"Would you like to order something John?"

"I'll have a mushroom burger and fries and a jumbo on tap."

"Anything more for you Pam?"

"No I'm all set thanks" Pam comments,

"A hamburger on a Friday night doesn't seem to fit the picture of a man engaged to be married John."

"Jill has a long ago planned dinner with her club at Chez Robert. It's her girl's night out".

"She seems to have a very active social life."

"That's true. Lately I've had so many events I can hardly keep up. Matter of fact it's tiring. I'm kind of worn out after a workday and I'd like a little time to relax in the evening. It's hard to party and have the obligatory adult beverages and then get up early and feel at your best."

"From my point of view you do it pretty well."

"Thank you for that but in my view that's in large part due to your efficiency in lining everything up for me and getting all those pleadings and motions done on time, even when I dictate a motion which has to be done for the next morning's continued trial. I mean it Pam. I want you to know I appreciate it. I know I asked a lot of you in the Bigg's trial and I planned on winning that case and having the money to share but we both know how that ended".

"You've got to stop acting as if that were the end of the world. I hate to see you work so hard and then be so disappointed because you didn't win. John you were a success. You presented a case just the way you planned, every bit of evidence went in the way you wanted. That was success. No lawyer can do more than that. You've proved your success in all the other cases you've tried also. The office is doing well financially. What is it in you that keeps you pushing for a big win and being so crushed if you don't reach that goal? Is money that important?"

John seems somewhat startled and Pam, seeing that, realizes she may have overstepped her bounds. After a brief pause she says,

"Oh I'm sorry. I guess I've overstepped my bounds. I have no right to get so personal."

"That's alright Pam. We've been together for a while now and you have a right to speak your mind and maybe I do need to look at the big picture as you say. It's just that where I stand right now is a turning point in my life. I'm about to marry into a family in which wealth plays an important part of their existence. I can't go into a situation where I'm a puppet to a dominant patriarch who would control me the way he does everything else. I doubt that Jill would accept a lifestyle that would be anything less than what she's accustomed to. I can't stand the thought of having to take money from her father. I can see him buying a house for us, one he thinks is suitable for his daughter. If we can't afford something she wants, he'll want to give it to her. If I accept it makes me subservient. If I refuse to allow it, then I'm the bad guy. So it's a lose-lose situation for me unless I can be successful enough to provide the life style she's comfortable with".

"The situation you describe has another option. If you love one another enough it would overcome the problem."

John looks at her as if her words are having an effect.

"Don't misunderstand me Pam, it's not that I want to live the life of an elitist. I'm not a snob. I never told you about my life. My father started running around with another woman. He divorced my mother and married the woman. Before that my father and mother had only rented a home and didn't have much. The support was intermittent. We went to live with my mother's family. The divorce wasn't her fault but it hurt her deeply that some blamed her. But she was courageous. She scraped together some money and went to beauty school. Then she started a beauty shop in another city with a friend she met in beauty school. We had no money to rent a home then. We lived in the back of the beauty shop, slept on a hide a bed and cooked on a hot plate. I learned to love canned tuna fish, rice and macaroni."

"The beauty shop was in a nice part of town and I played with the kids in the neighborhood. It was ok, but I still remember other kids teasing me and repeating `you haven't got a home to live in`".

"I went to a parochial school where divorced women were not looked upon kindly at that time, nor upon their children. My mother struggled with the business but we never went on welfare. Her business eventually became successful. I've always had a part time job since I was fourteen. I worked part time through high school and college. After college I worked full time and went to law school at night. I worked for an insurance company until I passed the bar. That's where I learned the personal injury business and dealt with wealthy lawyers. I guess that's what made me the way I am."

Pam is deeply touched. She puts her hand on John's hand and says, "John, there's nothing wrong with the way you are".

The waitress interrupts with the serving of food and Pam realizes what she's doing and quickly withdraws her hand.

"Don't let me interrupt anything but here's the mushroom burger and fries. Would either of you like something else?"

John and Pam look rather embarrassed. They speak together, stepping over the words of each other in their haste to say something to quickly change the idea that the waitress interrupted something that was going on between them.

"No…no nothing…tha… else…ank you."

The waitress leaves and John and Pam have an awkward moment where neither know what to say.

John, "Well the Conway trial…"

Pam, "Everything is ready…"

At that they laugh and smile at each other. John speaks,

"I wonder how the games coming along. Danny was telling me he hadn't scored a touchdown all season." Pam, who knows Danny's situation and likes him replies,

"He seems like an intelligent young man"'

"He is. He's very bright. His problem is he's looking for the wrong goals in his life."

"Really, it would be wonderful if we could all see what's best for us."

John's phone rings. He answers, listens and shows obvious concern.

"What happened? What was wrong? Is he ok? Where is he?

John cancels the call and says,

"I've got to go. That was Bob Conway, Danny's father. Danny was in a car accident. Bob says our team lost the game. Danny was involved in the last play of the game. He was in the open and in a position to score a winning touchdown. The pass was right to him and he dropped it. The team lost. Danny was crushed and couldn't be consoled."

All of this time John is signaling for the check, putting down the tip and paying the bill, rushing to get going. He continues to explain.

"Apparently Danny got into his car and rushed off, spinning his wheels and driving like a maniac. He got to highway 48 where he was going too fast for the curve and hit a tree. He's in critical condition at Mercy Hospital. I've got to go there. Do you want to come?"

"Yes. Let's go."

Chapter Five

John and Pam arrive at the hospital and are directed to intensive care. They find Bob Conway pacing back and forth. John asks,

"How is he doing?"

"He's suffered a fractured skull. The doctor thinks he has bleeding under his skull. They may have to operate to relieve pressure on his brain. He could die."

Bob stops talking as he is about to break into tears. He pauses for a moment and then says,

"I called his mother. She's on her way."

"Did you see him?"

"Yes, he was battered and bloody. He was unconscious. The last thing we talked about was the so called big game, as if that was the only important thing in life. Could those be the last words I said to him? Not how much I loved him and how proud I was of him for his scholastic achievements that I never had. Oh God, please don't let it be that I gave him the impression that the only important thing in life was catching a football."

"Bob, I think the charge weighed heavily on his mind. He felt terrible about being charged. Perhaps all that plus tonight's game was just too much pressure. But let's not focus on why it happened. Let's pray that he'll get better."

"When I called his mother she wanted to know why he was driving like that and I told her he had dropped that pass. She blamed me for putting so much emphasis on football. When she gets here I'll probably hear more of that."

Pam answered:

"I know Edith from our church Mr. Conway. I'm sure she'll be more concerned about Daniel's condition than placing blame. I'll do my best to console her....oh here's the doctor."

The doctor approaches the three of them and explains,

"We're prepping him for surgery now Mr. Conway. The MRI shows bleeding. We'll have to insert a tube into his skull to drain the blood and relieve any pressure on the brain and give the bleeding a chance to stop."

Bob turns away, covering his face in his hands.

John asks,

"How serious is the surgery?"

"The mechanics are not complicated. The important thing is for the bleeding to stop."

Bob pulls himself together and says,

"Thank you. Please help him." The doctor tries to assure him,

"Try not to worry. More likely than not he's going to come out of this and get back to normal."

"Oh he's got to, he's got to. I can't live with this."

Bob falls into his chair, bending over, head in his hands.

John thanks the doctor who then leaves. John says,

"Well I guess all we do now is wait"

Pam says,

"And pray."

Chapter Six

Next Monday is the day for Steve Sylvester's school board hearing. There are five members present at a table. Steve Sylvester sits at a table facing them. No one else is present. They shuffle papers and get things arranged. The chairman looks at every one and says,

"Everyone ready? Okay, let's begin. This is the hearing of the Montgomery School District board of directors regarding Steven Sylvester, a 12th grade teacher at Roosevelt High School with respect to the teaching of intelligent design. This board has received a complaint that teaching this theory violates the separation of church and state. Mr. Sylvester you were given due notice of the hearing and advised that you were to present your reasons for teaching that which has been alleged to be a creationist and therefore a religious doctrine. Are you prepared to present your reasons?"

"I am sir but first I would like to know who brought these charges against me. I believe I have a right to face my accuser or accusers." The chairman responds,

"I'm afraid that's not the case Mr. Sylvester. This is not a case of the accuser versus you but rather a situation where the board is being challenged to enforce a school policy. That policy prohibits the bringing of any religious teaching into the classroom."

"Then it's important for me to state right at the outset that I am not teaching a religious doctrine or bringing religion into the classroom. I'm simply pointing out obvious facts that can't be denied. Anyone can view those facts in any way they want and the purpose of science, a field to which I am totally devoted, is to put out all the facts and let anyone make their own conclusion. To do otherwise or to direct a student that he must accept one theory over another is anti-scientific. It's worse than that it's oppressive and dictatorial. So I'm telling this board that their premise is wrong."

"You are saying that I'm forcing students to accept religion when what I am doing is teaching undisputed facts and not making any conclusions as to what these facts prove. You on the other hand are saying that those facts lead one to make the conclusion that the facts prove a religion. So in fact it is you and the accusers who are making the conclusion, not me. The premise here is backward." The chairman is surprised by Steve's answer,

"Mr. Sylvester do you deny that teaching that the universe and our planets are carefully designed for human existence is in fact a presentation of the design of a creator?"

"I don't teach that it is carefully designed. I present the facts that there are at least 20 universal constants that are very delicately balanced such that if anyone of them were a nano fraction different, life on earth could not exist. Further, the odds against these factors being what they are, compared to what they could be, are like flipping a coin and having heads come up three hundred trillion times in a row. These are facts. These odds are so great that they are beyond the realm of chance. As a result scientists come to the conclusion that there must be multiple universes, each different, and we just happen to be in the one that is suitable to life. I tell my students of this multiple universe theory."

"But I also inform them that there is no evidence to support that theory. Now the difference is that I teach alternate theories but the accusers in this case refuse to allow any teaching other than their dogma. You should be holding a hearing on their close minded teaching."

The members are looking at each other, seeming confused and not knowing what to say.

Somewhat flustered the chairman says,

"Well, we've heard your position Mr. Sylvester. Does anyone else have any questions?"

No one responds.

"In that case thank you Mr. Sylvester. We'll consider the hearing closed. The board will consider what you've said and you will be advised of our decision in this matter. You are excused."

Steve thanks them and leaves the room. The board remains.

Chairman, "Well he certainly seems to know what he's talking about doesn't he?" Other members reply,

Member, "I'll say."

Other, "And there's no doubt he's very devoted."

Other, "He's actually a good teacher that knows what he's doing and why."

Other, "And he sticks to his principles as a true developer of young minds should. This is the type of man we want teaching our children."

Chairman, "He sticks to his principles." Then, changing his tone,

"Almost to the point of being stubborn."

Other, "(Acting subservient to the chairman) Yes, it's certainly hard to control an ideologue."

Other, "But there is a practical side of teaching that can't be ignored."

Other, (Seeing the direction things are going) "Our problem is that his ideals brought this issue to a head and the accusers swing a lot of authority in this community."

Other, "And control a lot of votes."

Chairman, "Gentlemen we can't let our concern for getting elected affect our opinion on this matter... on the other hand we are the board which sets school policy. After all we can't concede our authority to a person who works for us."

Other, "If we were perceived as being wishy-washy we'd soon lose all our authority. We have to let them know who is boss."

Chairman, "We were as much as told that if we don't do what they want this Women's Allegiance for Justice Group would file suit to enforce their claim

Other, "How did this come up? Who or what is this Women's Allegiance Group?"

Chairman, "They're an organization of activists looking for a lawsuit. They're an accident looking for a place to happen. They came to the school and demanded our high school curriculum and study lessons. You know what happens when these suits are filed. It always seems to be slanted in favor of the complainant and if the school board loses they have to pay damages and the attorney fees of the ones who filed the suit"

Other, "What did our initial investigation find?"

Chairman, "It found there was no basis for alleging the students were taught anything but well established science."

Other, "Did you show them the report?

Chairman, "Yes but they said that in federal courts intelligent design has almost exclusively been found to be a religious teaching. They said we shouldn't have done that investigation because it would show we were on the teacher's side and we should destroy all copies of the report unless we intend to fight them on this."

Other, "What did you do?"

Chairman, "I destroyed all reports. I think we should avoid getting sued by this activist group at all costs because those civil rights groups deliberately run up legal fees."

Other, "Congress created the problem. They set it up so that if the school board loses they pay the other side's attorney fees. And you know what happened in that suit over in Jefferson County. The civil rights group that filed the suit loaded it up with so many attorneys and written briefs that the school had to settle when they saw the attorney fee was going up to more than $300,000. It was just a matter of giving up to retain enough money to run the school."

Chairman, "Right. They paid the fees. If we were to support this teacher all the way through trial and appeal, the attorney bill for our side alone could be a half a million dollars, not to mention what it would be if we lost."

Other, "Let's be practical. Do you think the community would raise the school taxes just to support one man's stubborn adherence to an ideal?"

Chairman, "Let's face it, if he refuses to cease his manner of teaching, it's better that one man should lose his job than to face a situation where we wouldn't have enough money to operate a school and many teachers would lose their jobs."

Other, "If that happened Sylvester would be laid off anyway, so what's the difference?"

Chairman, "I think the answer is clear. Either the man ceases his teaching or he is terminated. It's settled then. We'll get a letter out to him in the morning."

Chapter Seven

The next day Pam is in the office when John walks in with his brief case. He says good morning to Pam, sets down his brief case, takes off his coat and hangs it on the coat rack. Pam responds,

"Morning John, how did it go this morning?"

"Well I got Danny's trial adjourned although it wasn't easy. Can you imagine Judge DeLato giving me a hard time adjourning the trial while Danny is still in the hospital recuperating from surgery?

"What did he want you to do, wheel him in in a hospital bed? Did you explain that he spent five days with a tube in his skull?"

"Yes and I gave him the doctor's report stating that even though it's been removed he's still too fragile to be going to trial. At that point he agreed with my request but he seemed so anxious to set the trial as soon as possible." Pam asks,

"Do you think he's feeling pressure from that Women's Alliance for Justice Group which has been pushing for easing law enforcement on criminals? They seem to have a powerful effect on voters and the judge does have to get re-elected"

John sits at his desk while Pam brings some typed papers to him. Then answers,

"I wouldn't want to think that it would affect his decision on the case but I suppose pressure by an outside group might make him want to move cases quickly. Anyway what time is Steve Sylvester coming in, he called me yesterday and said it was important to talk to me."

"He'll be here shortly. He was scheduled at 9:00 but I called him and told him you were in court and would be in about 10:30. He seemed anxious."

Steve Sylvester walks into the office entry door and Pam who was just going back to her desk after she spoke to John says,

"Oh, Mr. Sylvester. John is in and I believe he is ready to see you." She goes to John's office and nods that he's here.

"Send him in. Come in and have a seat Steve. Would you like some coffee?"

"No thanks John, I'm already hyper about this whole thing."

"Tell me about it. You said it had something to do with your job."

"Right. I told you the school board set up a hearing regarding my science class and what I teach the students. Well we had that meeting where I was accused of teaching intelligent design which they claim is bringing religion into the classroom. I told them I was only presenting accepted facts without making any conclusions but they didn't accept my defense and they fired me."

"I know the school board adopted a policy that no religious teaching could be brought into the class room based on the constitution which prohibits congress from establishing a religion. Actually what the founders had in mind was preventing the establishment of a particular religion such as the Church of England. They never meant that congress should take steps to abolish religion." Steve replies,

"I understand but since the advent of Darwinism the scientific community has become gradually convinced that a belief in religion is anti-scientific and it's gotten to the point where a cross on public land is the same as establishing a religion. That's where we are today."

"Steve I have to tell you that the law is pretty well settled when it comes to intelligent design. In the latest case that I know of a federal judge wrote a scathing opinion ridiculing intelligent design and determining that its main purpose was to indoctrinate students into a religious belief. I don't think it was a well-reasoned decision because he rejected the testimony of experts in favor of intelligent design who were every bit as well qualified as those who testified against it. He rejected their testimony solely because they were prevented from publishing their papers by a majority who refuse to consider their position. So what I'm telling you, unfortunately, is that your chances of winning a lawsuit are very unlikely."

"But I'm not doing anything but presenting well accepted facts. Facts that can't be explained away by theories. John, theories are nothing more than supposition. Evolution is based on suppositions John. It's all about what *could* have happened. Those who propound such theories don't have any better basis to accept them than any other theory. I could explain to you why they don't and you would see that there's no basis for teaching them as dogma."

John at this point John sees little hope in taking the case, knowing that in federal courts the issue is essentially dead. He tells Steve,

"But you also have to consider the cost of hiring experts. Expert testimony is expensive and the law is pretty much against you. Steve, in considering a case like this you have to weigh the costs of hiring experts and the likely hood of success."

"Well maybe the school wouldn't be able to afford hiring such experts either. John this isn't just an argument about theories, it's my life. I've got a family to support. I don't have any prospects for a job. I can't even promise you I'd have the money to pay for expensive experts. But I can educate you on this subject. If you take the time to work with me I can convince you that my position is fair and has just as solid a foundation as those who oppose it."

John decided to give Steve time to possibly accept the inevitable.

"I'll tell you what Steve, before we get into any long instructional sessions, write me a summary just as you would in presenting an essay. I'll take a look at it."

"Thanks John, I can't ask anything more."

They shake hands. Steve leaves and says goodbye to Pam.

Chapter Eight

Steve was prompt in getting his summary to John and several days later John is in his office with piles of books around him as he researches the issue of what factors the courts consider with regard to the issue of separation of church and state. As he studies Pam enters his office.

"Here's that case you wanted to see. How is your research coming along?

"You know what just occurred to me? What's odd is that all the federal cases I've been studying involve a violation of the establishment clause of the constitution."

John is walking around, thinking out loud as he has just thought of a way to keep the case out of federal court and put the case in a different perspective.

"This case is different. It's basically a civil suit for improper firing which has nothing to do with the constitution. It's a violation of his employment contract. Yet the case hinges on a religious interpretation so in one sense it's similar but it's really a totally different theory. You know what that means? It means that all of the settled law on intelligent design which is based on the constitution doesn't apply. That means we're breaking new ground which is good for Steve's case but we still have to prove that intelligent design is not a religious teaching. That's an awful lot of technical testimony which will take expensive expert testimony. You know Steve can't afford that expense so I'll have to advance the costs with little chance of being repaid."

Pam, sensing his enthusiasm, says, "Do you think we have enough in the till to afford financing that?"

"You're right Pam when you said 'we'. There could be pay less paydays for both of us."

Pam, who privately believes that federal courts overstep their bounds when it comes to religion, has faith in John's intellect and ability and is weighing what it would mean for her to have to take a cut in pay as opposed to the pleasure of seeing federal courts stopped from meddling in an area where they don't belong. That is if he were successful. She didn't have to think very long. She said,

"I'm for it if you are John".

John said excitedly,

"Sounds like the games on."

Chapter Nine

At the same time in Gregg Stryker's home Greg is leading a man, Henry Cobb, who is the court clerk to Judge DeLato, to a chair in his living room.

"Have a seat Henry. Would you like a drink?"

"No thanks Gregg. I've got to get back to court after lunch." Gregg hands Henry an envelope.

"Well here's the 'commission' I owe you for your good work in that Gibbs trial. This will be enough for your share and that jury foreman. I trust you'll be discreet in your dealings with him. How did you manage to get your man into the foreman position?"

"I'm the one who picks the jury pool and this man is a good speaker that I knew would be picked as foreman with the ability to influence the jury." Henry looks at the cash and puts it in his pocket. "Just out of curiosity why was it important to you for Taylor to lose that case?"

"It was mostly for General Contracting. I have a lot of dealings with them. I was planning to do an addition to my plant and needless to say I got a really good price. Also as a bonus I thought if Taylor would lose he might give up on his ambitions to be a big trial lawyer and take a secure job as a prosecutor. It was two birds with one stone so to speak."

"Understood…. I've got to get back to court. The judge is a stickler for being on time. If he had any idea of what we're up to he'd try to put us all in jail. But since we're equally involved I don't see anyone letting any of it get out."

"Right, just make sure all dealings are in cash." He leads Henry to the door.

"No problem. See you later, bye".

At the same time just as Henry is leaving a young man, Chris Ott, comes to the door, almost bumps into Henry and says,

"Oh excuse me, I was just coming to talk to Mr. Stryker. I'm from the Hilltown Post. I'm doing a story on the expansion of the Stryker plant and I'd like to have an interview with you Mr. Stryker. I'm sorry I almost bumped into you Mr. Cobb." Henry thinks nothing about it and replies,

"No problem. I recognize you. You're the new reporter who covers legal cases occasionally for the Post." Gregg interjects,

"Well I usually expect the press to make an appointment in advance but as long as you're here you may as well come in."

"Thank you sir."

Henry leaves with a nod to Gregg. They go into the living room and sit. Gregg offers him a drink which he declines. Then Greg explains,

"Henry was just here to bring me a copy of the city's plot plan for the factory's property just as a favor to save me a trip."

"Yes. I guess he got to see me sitting in the court room during the Biggs trial. It was my first assignment when I started working for the Post."

"Oh you watched that trial, then you saw my future son in law in action. Too bad he wasn't successful." Chris agrees and offers his opinion,

"Right, I thought he did a good job. I had a write up prepared for the paper but when he didn't get a judgment it was a non-story. The way the evidence went in I thought he should have won and I tried to interview some of the jurors but most of them just took my number and promised to call me. So far none of them has."

"Well there's no sense in digging into that. It's old history. Now what is it you want to know about our plant expansion?"

Chapter Ten

That afternoon John met Jill for lunch at Bradford's. The two were chatting as were the other patrons in the restaurant. It is a pleasant place with mahogany tables with white table cloths, cloth napkins and wood paneled walls. The waiter brings their food. He is very proper, subservient, obsequious, wanting to please.

"There you are sir, the choice was excellent. Please enjoy."

They begin to eat and John says,

"So let me tell you about an interesting case I've decided to take regarding a science teacher at Roosevelt High who's been wrongfully terminated."

"Is this going to be the big verdict you've been hoping for John? I hope so although I can't see why you won't take daddy's help and run for prosecutor. It may not pay bundles of money but it's prestigious."

"Let's not get into that again. You know how I feel about that job."

"I know, I know. But why is it so important for you to become independently wealthy. There'll be plenty of money when we're married." Mentioning her father's money irritates John.

"Do you think I want to live my life on your father's money? And who says I am taking this case just for money?"

"Well John you talk about the money and prestige that go along with being a big trial lawyer. What am I supposed to think?

"I didn't realize I gave that impression." John pauses, then says thoughtfully, "Maybe I have been giving too much thought about the money and prestige. It just seemed to me that that is the ultimate goal of any lawyer's career. Anyway this case isn't the type that will lead to great financial rewards or prestige, Steve Sylvester hardly has an extra dime to pay my fee but he is so passionate about what he thinks is right."

Jill seems visually shaken when she hears the teacher's name and asks,

"Is Steve Sylvester the teacher you're going to represent?"

"Yes do you know him?"

"Oh no, no but I recognize the name. It came up in a conversation the other day." John asks,

"How could anyone that you know, know anything about him that would come up in a conversation. What was the conversation about?"

"Oh I can't remember what it was about. It's nothing, nothing at all?"

"Ok, anyway I think this case has an interesting issue. From Steve's point of view it's the school board suppressing scientific facts. From the school's point of view Steve is teaching religion." Jill reveals more of her true feelings by saying,

"He's teaching religion by teaching intelligent design?" Which requires more explanation.

"Yes how did you know?"

"You said he was a science teacher. My understanding of intelligent design is that it promotes scientific facts to suggest that our world was designed."

"You seem to know a lot about this subject. I didn't know you were into science."

"As if ID could be called science." Which heats the discussion up even more.

"Whoa, it sounds like you're not the person I want on my jury."

"John I don't think you should take this case. You're going to be trying to convince people of a dark age's philosophy. You'll be ridiculed. That reflects on me,"

"That may be a barrier I have to overcome but it's nothing that you have to get involved with although I would expect a little more support from my fiancé."

"I can't support you on this. John, you're not to take this case." Jill's bossiness is too much.

"Where is it written that you decide what cases I take and which I don't?"

"You don't think I have any say in what do and how it affects me?"

"Do you think you have the right to tell me how to run my business? And you think I'm self-centered just because I claim the right to think for myself?"

John is speaking loudly now and people are beginning to notice. Jill replies,

"I'm insisting you don't take that case and I'm not going to sit here and let you yell at me. I'm leaving." Jill walks out angrily.

The other patrons in the restaurant observed the entire event and saw nothing humorous about a couple having a public disagreement until…

John sat there, fuming, for a few moments, as the waiter comes out of the kitchen totally unaware of what had taken place. He sees the unfinished food and says,

"Oh dear, the lady didn't like her food. Shall I wrap it up for you sir?

John slams down the money for the bill and says loudly,

"Perhaps I'm the one who should wrap it up". He storms out.

The waiter stands there with Jill's plate in his hand in total confusion, looking left and right, and wondering why people are laughing.

Chapter Eleven

The next morning John visits Danny at the hospital. Danny is sitting in a chair next to his bed.

"It's so nice of you to keep visiting me Mr. Taylor. I'm beginning to feel normal."

"You were lucky Danny. You could have been killed."

"It was foolish of me to get so upset about a dropped catch, I know. But I had wanted so badly to make a difference in that game. I wanted to feel important. When I dropped it, it was like I had lost everything I hoped to be. I felt I had let down my dad."

"Do you know how much your dad loves you and how bad he felt when he thought that he had pushed you into this whole football business?"

"Mr. Taylor I know how he felt. We had a good talk and a good cry. I'm alright with it now. I realize that a football game and being a hero really isn't the most important thing in life."

"I think you're fortunate to have learned such an important lesson at your age Danny. Some of us take much later in life to come to our senses. You've got a good brain in that head Danny. You're going to be successful in whatever career you chose... as long as it's not football."

Danny laughs and says,

"I hope you're right sir. As of now I've missed a lot of school but the teachers are bringing me assignments and my dad has hired tutors so hopefully I won't be delayed in graduating."

"Danny, I've come to bring you some news. You will want to think it over and talk to your mom and dad about it. I've talked to the prosecutor. In view of your accident and injuries he's willing to accept a plea of nolo contendere. If the judge accepts it you will get six months' probation and under the Morgan Youthful Offender law the conviction will be expunged from your record after you turn 21 with no more offenses. That means there will be no convictions on your record. It's a good deal. The other condition is that after you graduate you must be employed. I've talked to the doctor and he feels that it would be best for you."

"Oh that would be a great relief Mr. Taylor. I'll talk to mom and dad but I want to accept. The only problem is I have no job prospects at this point."

"I can help you Danny. I've taken on a case for Mr. Sylvester versus the school board and it's going to take a lot of research, especially in science. I know you're good on computers and if you're willing I'd like to hire you to help me in doing this research. I'll tell you what I need and you find it for me. Would you like to do that?"

"Would I? Wow, that's so cool, doing research in a real case. I'd love to do it. Thank you."

"Then it's a deal. When do you think you'll be ready to start?"

"Just get me a computer and I'm ready right now."

"We'll let's not rush anything. I'll check with you parents and if they approve, when you're ready, you'll get that computer."

Pam comes in. John and Pam had discussed this previously and John tells her,

"Hi Pam. Meet your new assistant. He seems anxious to get started."

"Hi Danny, I'm glad you can help us. We're going to need it. I've just got the witness list filed by the school board attorney.

They've hired a defense firm from Chicago and listed enough expert witnesses to snow us under." John asks,

"How is the school board going to afford that firm and the expense of all those expert witnesses? There's something going on that we don't know about. They've got someone or some group to finance them. I wonder who?"

Chapter Twelve

The Chicago lawyer, Creighton Harding, is in the office he set up in town. The office is bare, with only necessary equipment. Creighton is six feet tall with a round face and sandy colored hair which he combs straight back. He exudes confidence, some would call it arrogance. He has an associate lawyer working with him who is at his desk reading cases and making notes. A secretary sits at another desk, typing. The phone rings, she answers and buzzes Creighton,

"It's your boss calling from Chicago"

"Hi Alan, how are things back in Chicago?" He listens. "Good. Yes, we're making progress. Depositions are scheduled. I expect them to go well. We've got our expert witnesses lined up. Dr. Adler is an experienced witness and has good credentials. We've used him before and he's smooth and reliable." Creighton listens and responds,

"I think the jury will believe him as opposed to the plaintiff's expert witnesses. Adler has published a lot as opposed to the plaintiff witnesses." He listens again and responds. "I know, I know they are respected scientists but their views on intelligent design don't get published because they're not in the majority. I don't care how logical their points are, I'll make them appear foolish and out of touch and I'll do the same with that self-righteous teacher, Sylvester. I'll make it look like he's only interested in getting money." Creighton listens again. "Yes we've already loaded them down with interrogatories and requests for admissions. That Taylor guy has a single practice. He'll be so busy responding to us that he'll hardly have time to prepare for trial. Yes sir, don't worry I'll show him what it's like to play in the major league. Ok, all right I'll keep in touch."

"Creighton hangs up and says to his associate, "Have you been able to dig up any dirt on Sylvester? Anything we can use to bring him down in the eyes of the jury?"

"Not yet, I've got an investigator on it. He tells me that in a town this size the people are pretty closed mouthed to any stranger. But we'll keep working on it."

"Make sure you do. I want to grind these people into the dust and get back to the big city. So far what do we know about this Taylor guy?" His associate answers,

"He's tried a lot of cases locally with some success except for one big loss.. He's engaged to Jill Stryker. She's the secretary/treasurer of the Women's Alliance for Justice which oddly enough seems to have some kind of a relationship with our client, the school board. She's also the daughter of Gregg Stryker."

Creighton responds,

"It sounds like our man Taylor is going to marry into money. Is he a social climber?"

"Not really. From what I hear he is driven to make a lot of money but only by making it himself".

"I wonder why he's taken this case. It's not going to be a big money winner. Is he becoming altruistic?"

"You mean doing something just because it's the right thing to do? If he is it would mean his goals are changing which seems unlikely"

"Well we'll see what we can do to prevent him from changing into a 'do gooder'." Both laugh.

The secretary buzzes Creighton and says,

"There's a Jill Stryker on the phone for you Mr. Harding. She says she wants to make an appointment to talk to you."

"By all means put her on!"

"Mr. Harding I'm Jill Stryker. I'm the secretary/ treasurer for the Women's Alliance for Justice. Perhaps you don't know it but we are very interested in supporting the school district in this lawsuit. We have invested money in the case and we have prepared a file with our investigation and some research on the law which we think will help you with the case. If you would like I'll have it sent to you by courier or if you want to talk further I can bring it to you."

"That sounds wonderful. Why don't we meet for lunch? How about tomorrow at noon?"

"Fine. We can meet at the country club. I'll send a driver to pick you up."

"Great, see you then."

Chapter Thirteen

Four weeks have passed, seemingly with the speed of light, and the Sylvester trial date is getting close. John is in his office with books stacked all over his desk. Danny is in the reception area to the left of Pam's desk where he sits at a desk with a computer. John has a stack of case reports on his desk. Frank walks in, Pam and Danny say hello. Frank is 34, jovial in nature, five feet eight and rotund. Contrary to Frank, John is more serious in demeanor, but the way his lips automatically fall into a smile prevent the impression that he's irascible.

Frank responds to Pam and Danny and, as usual, helps himself to a cup of coffee. He knocks quietly and enters John's office saying,

"I thought I'd drop in to see how your Sylvester case is coming along. I know you've been doing constant depositions. I hardly see you at the Bench and Bar anymore."

"I know, that silk stocking firm from Chicago has a partner and an associate working on burying us in discovery requests and motions. This must be costing the school board plenty. I can't understand where they plan to get the money to afford all those legal costs."

"Yeah that's an interesting question John. Where do you stand now with the case?" John knows the issues so well he can readily summarize,

"I've filed a wrongful discharge case in state court contending the school fired Steve without valid reason. The school board claims they had a valid reason to fire him because he was promoting religion which is against school policy. So the principal issue in the case is whether the school had a valid reason to determine he was teaching religion. The issue is simply whether or not he was teaching religion. If I can convince judge DeLato it's a factual issue we can get past a summary judgment and have a jury trial."

"I'm not into this issue John, how does intelligent design translate into teaching religion? Does it flat out state that there is a creator?"

"That's the thing. It doesn't teach there's a creator but it presents facts that are scientifically known which tend to make the beginning of life seem miraculous. Even the beginning of the universe was miraculous. Don't doubt me on this even though it seems impossible but the best scientific evidence proves that the universe exploded out of nothing. Absolutely nothing. And if you don't believe me Steve will show you the statements of the most respected scientists in the world to confirm it. Steve has taught me a lot I didn't know."

"Alright so the universe popped into existence billions of years ago due to some unknown phenomenon. That still doesn't prove that there was a creator." Frank responds logically.

"True, but there are certain factors, they call them universal constants. I'm talking about things such as gravity, the speed of light, the force that holds atoms together and so on. There are about twenty of them that are precisely balanced such that if they weren't exactly where they are life couldn't exist. Now don't get confused and blank out on me. You don't have to know what each of these constants is but the point is they are constant throughout the universe. Let's take one that you know very well, gravity. It is of universal strength throughout the universe with regard to its relation to mass." John continues to explain,

"Please understand this. There is nothing that says that gravity's strength has to be where it is. Let's assume hypothetically it could be a strength of anywhere from 0 to ten.

And that our gravity is set, not only at 4 on that hypothetical scale, it is set at 4.379597643865. I'm using hypothetical numbers but the point is that its actual verified setting is 12 units beyond the decimal point and if it were not that precise, life as we know it could not exist. Think about the odds of gravity being set that precisely by chance. Each of the numbers from one to ten has at least 12 units beyond the whole number so that's thirteen factors times ten increasing the odds for each of the ten numbers."

"Multiplying ten time thirteen, it means there are one hundred and thirty possibilities on the hypothetical scale we're using where gravity could be set. Now multiply the number of possibilities for each of the other nineteen universal constants. Take the speed of light, think how many variables there are for the speed of light which is eighteen million kilometers per minute. Think how many variables there are considering **all** twenty constants? All of which must be set where they are for life to exist."

"An Oxford mathematician calculated the odds using the actual scientific variables and established the exact odds at 10 to the 1023rd power against the universe happening by chance. That's such a large number that it is considered scientifically impossible. Scientists do not say that anything is possible, they have a standard which limits the range of possibilities. That number far exceeds the scientific realm of possibility."

"Those are impressive numbers Johnny, but do you think you can get a jury to understand that?"

"They will if they can understand that the odds of the universe happening by chance are greater than flipping a coin and having it come up heads three hundred million times in a row."

"There are about twenty of these constants and the odds of things happening like that are so enormously against it that you logically have to rule out chance. So if it wasn't by chance do we conclude it was made to sustain human life?" Frank continues testing John's theory,

"Are there any other possibilities explaining the origin of the universe, and please understand John, you're talking to a guy who didn't even know the universe had a beginning."

"Well there are other possibilities if you want to consider theories without any evidence to support them. For some reason scientists prefer other possibilities. For instance you can reduce the odds against the universe being so perfectly balanced for life by theorizing that there are multiple universes. The odds are probably about 300 million to one against it happening but you can make the odds more favorable if you say there must be 300 million different universes and ours happened to be the one with all the settings just right for life. "

"Are you telling me there are scientists who believe in multimillion universes?"

"Yes, seriously. And others feel they might exist in other dimensions which we can't see….Look I don't have a problem with others having their theories. Maybe they are as valid as intelligent design. But I see Steve's position. You shouldn't prevent any reasonable possibility from being presented and letting the person make up his or her own mind as to what makes most sense. There is no evidence of multiple universes but there is evidence of intelligence."

"I see what you're saying, let everyone believe whatever theory seems most reasonable to them. But the intelligent design theory seems to require belief in a miraculous creation,"

"Well if science has proved that the universe popped out of nothing hasn't it already proved that there are miracles by their definition?" Frank concedes that John has made his point,

"Touché ole buddy. You can win the argument with me but you and I both know that when it comes to cross examining an expert in their own field you're walking through a minefield."

"I know and that's where this case will soar or crash. All I can say is I hope I'm up to the challenge."

"You've got my vote pal. Well I'll leave these sophisticated and noble arguments to you. My days are spent on simply trying to prove he or she didn't do it. Most of my clients feel that if they can't figure out how to steal it, it doesn't exist in their minds. See you later."

Chapter Fourteen

Jill Stryker is in the office of the Woman's Alliance for Justice meeting with Agnes Sparrow, the mid-western district director of the WAJ. Also present is the president of the local and another member. Agnes is a domineering woman, tall black haired with a long roman nose and wearing heavy mascara giving the appearance of sunken eyes, and with the prominent nose, almost that of a beak, she almost looks like a raven. Jill introduces her to the other members and after pleasantries Agnes says,

"What do you think of this lawyer the school board has hired?"

"I met with him last week. He seems confident, almost arrogant. We discussed the case and he is well aware of the issues. He presents himself well. If you can believe him he's had many successful trials including several involving the constitutional issue regarding the separation of church and state."

"He better be good he's running up an enormous bill. I want you to understand Ms. Stryker that we are your parent organization and we have decided to help the school board finance their defense in this lawsuit. We are doing so because this teacher has presented a strong case for intelligent design. When we received your copy of the school board's internal investigation we realized that he was cleverly presenting his teachings in a more or less factual manner which, if found to be legal, could upset all the work we've accomplished in keeping any thought of religion out of the minds of our future generations. You are not aware of the effort and years we have been working on this through the federal courts and the Supreme Court to the point where we've got all the federal courts ruling that intelligent design is a religious teaching. And now here is this case wherein the foolish school board did an internal investigation showing that this so called teacher is doing nothing but presenting facts and which report could give this Taylor fellow a free ticket to win his case."

Agnes reaches for the WAJ file on the case.

"Is this the copy of your file in this matter?"

"Yes, but we told the school board to destroy that report and they did. So there are no copies left of that report."

"Except this one which is contained in your file. Why wasn't that destroyed also?"

"We try to keep a complete investigation and there's no way that that report will get in the hands of John Taylor,"

"You said you gave Creighton Harding a copy of your file, was this report in the copy you gave him?"

"I assume that report was not copied and even if it was, why would Creighton give it to John Taylor?"

"You assume, you assume? I'm sure John Taylor has used discovery to request copies of all of the school board's file and Mr. Harding is not going to risk his career by hiding discoverable material so by now he's probably decided to give it to Taylor."

Agnes continues angrily,

"All this effort we've put into preventing the next generation from gaining any access to a religious belief is going to be gone if Taylor wins this case. How could you make such a mistake? For more than 3000 years the world's greatest thinkers have envisioned a society ruled in perfect justice by the leading intellectuals of the time so that equality will be spread throughout the working class. I'm talking about Plato's Republic, Sir Thomas Moore's Utopia, Locke and on down the line. People can't rely on their bibles and fairy tales for justice. Their trust must be in science and intellectual men and here you are giving teachers like this Sylvester fellow a foot hold to bring back religion into the schools. I'm telling you Ms. Stryker if Taylor wins this case you will regret it."

Jill, visibly shaken, replies,

"Ms. Sparrow, I will assure you that John Taylor will not win this case no matter what has to be done to stop him. Trust me on this, we have methods to use if we have to that will assure that our side will win."

"You better be sure Ms. Stryker. You better be."

Chapter Fifteen

A few days before John was in his office in the morning and found on his desk a large white envelope from Creighton. John reached for his letter opener and eagerly opened the package. He was surprised to find a document entitled 'Supplemental Answer to Plaintiff's Interrogatories'. He knew that the time for formal discovery had expired and from his prior experience with Creighton, getting any information from him was like pulling teeth. Now he had a package of information given to him freely. He noted there was an attachment labeled Exhibit A. When he read it he couldn't believe his eyes. It was a copy of an investigation report by the school board which found that Steve Sylvester did not engage in any activity promoting religion to his students. It was a bolt from the blue, manna from heaven. This was an admission from the school board that completely supported Steve's case. He felt with this he could win his case on a motion before the judge without the bother of a jury trial. Up to this point he was preparing a response to Creighton's motion for Summary Judgment which meant that Steve's case could be thrown out by the judge on the basis that all evidence showed that Steve's teaching was in fact promoting religion. Now he had the evidence to support Steve's case and defeat Creighton's motion.

John hurried to prepare an emergency motion and schedule it at the same time as Creighton's motion for summary judgment.

Four days later Creighton was in judge DeLato's courtroom, waiting for John to show up. Only the clerk, Henry Cobb, and the court reporter are present, each on opposite sides of the judge's bench. The clerk is working with papers. Creighton walks up to the clerk and says,

"I'm here on the Sylvester case. Is Taylor here yet?"

Clerk, "Not yet."

Creighton responds in a sarcastic voice, "Maybe he's come to his senses and intends to dismiss the case before the judge does."

Mr. Cobb does not respond but picks up some papers and walks into the judge's chamber through a door which he closes behind him. Creighton sits down at the counsel table and puts papers onto the table as John comes in.

"Thought you might not make it."

"Why would you think that?"

"Look John, I've read your brief. There's not one case that's favorable to you. It's clear that ID is a religious teaching and the school was justified in terminating your client for violating policy."

"Save your argument for the judge, Creighton, you're not going to convince me."

The judge enters the court room and the clerk announces,

"Hear ye, hear ye. The Circuit Court of Montgomery County is now in session. The case of Sylvester versus Montgomery County School Board is before the court. Judge DeLato presiding."

"Please be seated. Good morning gentlemen. Is there anything else before we proceed with the motion?"

John replies,

"Yes your honor. I've prepared an emergency motion to reopen discovery in order to follow up on this new found report which has just been given to me by Mr. Harding after the closing of discovery. Your honor this report, which was an investigation done by the school board, clearly states that Mr. Sylvester was not using his position as a teacher to promote religion. The report says that he was teaching generally accepted factual material. Your honor this report is a blockbuster. It's an admission by the defendant that our claim is justified. I need to have further depositions to find out who did this investigation and why it was delayed and not given to me until after discovery was closed."

"Why was it delayed so long Mr. Harding?"

"It was filed away and not found until recently your honor. I gave it to counsel as soon as it was found. But it doesn't matter your honor. This report was nothing more than a conclusion made by an independent person who was not authorized by the school board to make any conclusions on behalf of the board. This is an unauthorized opinion of a lay parson who has no standing to issue an opinion on critical matters in this case. The facts related in the report are hearsay from other persons whom I have not had the opportunity to cross examine. Allowing the jury to read such a report from an unauthorized lay person would be extremely prejudicial to my client. Mr. Taylor had the opportunity to depose the plaintiff's students and get firsthand information but instead he's trying to rely on hearsay testimony to do his work for him. He wants to reopen the discovery and delay the trial to go on a fishing expedition at this late date and I object your honor."

John attempts to reply,

"Your honor I..."

Judge DeLato interrupts,

"Counsel I tend to agree with Mr. Harding that it is hearsay and an unwarranted opinion and I do not want to delay this trial. Therefore, Mr. Taylor, your motion to reopen discovery is denied."

John is stunned and Creighton is jubilant.

"I've read your briefs, Mr. Harding, this is your motion for summary disposition, please proceed."

"Thank you your honor. As I have pointed out in my brief the school board, in accord with federal law, has a policy to prohibit any teaching that promotes a religion. It's clear that the plaintiff herein is promoting an anti-evolution program that points out the supposed false premises of Darwinism in an effort to convince his students of his admitted religious beliefs."

"What specific points do you rely on counsel?"

Creighton points out to the judge that John claims that in the Cambrian period a plethora of new life formed in a relatively brief period of time. He points out that certain complex systems such as blood clotting or eyesight cannot have developed gradually since these systems would be useless in a partially developed form and therefore must have occurred all at once pursuant to a design. Your honor the conclusion he is promoting is that there is a creator. All of this goes to support the defendant's position that the plaintiff is violating the prohibition of a public support of a religion".

The judge replies,

"I've read your expert witnesses' affidavit counsel. I note Dr. Adler claims that evolution is a fact. Did I miss something counsel, has the so called missing link been discovered? It seems to me that over the years I've heard a lot of talk about the missing link which led me to believe that something was needed to finalize the concept."

"According to Dr. Adler scientists are confident that a missing link between ape and man will eventually be found your honor. He has so testified."

"But as I read Dr. Adler's affidavit he states evolution is a fact. Perhaps we need a valid definition of what is a fact as we proceed in this court room counsel."

"Your honor Dr. Adler's credentials are impeccable. Plaintiff's experts who support Mr. Sylvester's position are not accepted by the majority of scientists in the field. Their papers are not published in scientific journals."

"You say the majority of scientists don't accept that position. Are you admitting counsel that there are a minority of scientists who support plaintiff's position in this case? As a general rule of law courts are established to allow both sides of an issue and not exclude ideas just because they are not in the majority. In jurisprudence we like to allow reason and not numbers to rule."

"I can only say that Dr. Adler's testimony is that their position is not accepted by the majority."

John notices that the judge seems displeased with Creighton's answer. The judge continues,

"I note that in his deposition Dr. Adler made the statement that the scientific method requires observation and demonstration. He also says that only natural causes can be considered in the study of science. I find that quite interesting. Has anyone observed an actual real life evolutionary change or been able to duplicate it in the laboratory?

"Well your honor any change that took place was eons ago so there are only the fossils to study and of course no one can duplicate a change of species in the laboratory."

"I understand that no one has been able to create life in the laboratory, is that true Mr. Harding?"

"It is your honor.

"Was the beginning of life considered a natural or unnatural event Mr. Harding?" Creighton answers,

"I understand that it is currently not known how organic life could begin from only inorganic matter. It can't be considered a natural event." Judge DeLato reasons,

"I would adduce therefore that until a natural event is found it is currently considered an unnatural event but according to Dr. Adler no cause other than a natural cause can be considered because science doesn't go there, is that correct?"

"That's correct."

"Well, if scientists consider the beginning of life an unnatural cause and they are still searching to find a natural cause then how can Dr. Adler claim as a fact that life evolved if they cannot demonstrate a natural cause? If I understand Mr. Taylor's position the implication of ID is that there is an unnatural cause for the existence of man and his position is that valid scientists are looking into facts that support that position. It seems to me that they are both looking into the same thing and that neither has reached a conclusion. How do you explain the difference Mr. Harding?"

This is a difficult position for even the best of lawyers to be in but Creighton is good at thinking on his feet. After an uncomfortable pause he says,

"Well I suppose the scientists are trying to find a way to explain it without getting into religion and the ID proponents are trying to prove a religion and that is why their teaching violates the school boards regulations."

"What about that Mr. Taylor? Are the proponents of ID proposing an answer that only permits a conclusion that God created life?"

Now the ball is in John's court, putting him in the same position that Creighton was in a moment ago. He is faced with overcoming the supposition that everyone has made, i.e. that if it wasn't natural it had to be miraculous and therefore created by God which would create the conclusion that the theory is religious and would automatically defeat his case. Creighton senses this and turns toward John, emphasizing the importance of his answer and thinking that this will put an end to the case. But John is also good at thinking on his feet and he replies,

"Intelligent design proposes an intelligent cause your honor. That neither presupposes nor disproves the existence of God for it only gives credence to intelligence. It does not presume that human beings are the only possessors of intelligence. Dr. Stephen Hawking, probably the world's most renowned cosmologist and theoretical physicist, has written that life was brought to earth by alien beings who presumably are exceptionally more intelligent than mankind. His opinion has not been ridiculed but rather given respect as a theory." John continues,

"So it demonstrates that that there are other possible intelligences and therefore ID does not point to only one conclusion. Therefor the defendant's basic presumption that ID points only to a deity is fallacious and that the basis of his motion to dismiss fails."

Judge DeLato asks,

"Have you heard of Dr. Hawking counsel?" Creighton nods. "I understand that Dr. Hawking is perhaps the most honored cosmologist in modern times counsel yet he has written that in his opinion life was brought to earth by alien beings, have you read his writings counsel?"

Creighton nods that he has, looking puzzled.

"Would that be a natural or unnatural cause counsel?"

"I'm not a qualified cosmologist your honor but if the earth were populated by beings from outer space I would think that would be a natural cause as opposed to an unnatural or supernatural cause."

"Mr. Harding, if serious scientists are willing to consider the existence of aliens from outer space but not the existence of unnatural causes that strike me as inconsistent and unfair because I don't think there is anything natural about alien beings who themselves have never been proven. Here's my point. You say that if Darwinism cannot at this stage designate what can be considered a natural cause. But science won't consider an unnatural cause even though they will accept a visit from aliens with the apparent altruistic purpose of populating the earth. Which it seems to me is close to the epitome of an unnatural cause. In addition to that I think it is apparent that this case presents a classical picture of conflicting facts which by their very nature preclude a summary disposition. Do you have anything to add Mr. Taylor?"

"Nothing to add your honor."

"Good. Now here's where we stand gentlemen. This is a wrongful termination case and a jury trial. Because of the unusual circumstances of this case religion has become an issue. It must be determined if what Mr. Sylvester teaches is an attempt to introduce religion into the school curricula. Defendant claims through its expert testimony that Darwinism is established by facts. Plaintiff claims that the facts he teaches challenge that theory and show that there are various ways of demonstrating intelligence design without a deity. Therefore it is apparent that there is a conflict of facts which must be determined by a jury. As you know in a motion to dismiss I am to consider the facts of the case in the light most favorable to the party opposing the motion. That in itself prevents me from ruling in your favor Mr. Harding and I intend to allow a fair consideration of the facts in this case. Motion denied. And now that discovery and motions are completed, I've just had a trial settle which opens an earlier date for this case. I'm going to move this trial up to March 15th, just over one week from now. I expect you both to be ready at that time. Good afternoon gentlemen."

Chapter Sixteen

Pam is praising John who is back in the office after defeating Creighton's motion to dismiss.

"John you did it. The judge is going to let the case go to the jury." She says with admiration

"You're a winner John, a dynamite lawyer."

"Come on Pam, if you had looked closer you would have seen that I was sweating bullets to answer the judge's question. But I do admit that seeing the look on Creighton's face was worth more than money. After the judge's ruling he stammered and couldn't seem to get a word out. Of course there's nothing he could say. The judge was definite in his ruling. Now we have to hurry to get ready for the trial which is just ten days away."

Danny rushes in with a newspaper in his hand.

"Hey, were in the news. The judge's decision was picked up by the national news. Look at this headline. He shows the newspaper: **JUDGE RULES THERE IS A GOD**

"What? Let me see that." John takes the newspaper and reads, "In a circuit court hearing this morning Judge DeLato of Montgomery County Circuit Court issued a decision contrary to many previous multi state rulings. The judge's decision would allow a jury to determine that there is a God if the jury believes the evidence presented by the plaintiff in the case of Sylvester v. The Montgomery School Board. The case involves a school teacher who was fired for allegedly promoting religion to his science class students. John Taylor, the plaintiff's attorney, argued that factual teachings can be shown to support the plaintiff's position'. That headline is very misleading."

Danny comments,

"Misleading or not the afternoon edition is selling fast and furious. I bet it will be on the evening news."

John replies,

"Don't put it past a reporter to stretch the facts a little to create a sensation."

The phone rings and Pam answers it.

"Hello." She listens. "Yes Mr. Harding, hold on please."

"John it's Creighton Harding. He wants to talk to you."

"Hello, this is John. Yes, Creighton, thank you." He listens… "You can try to appeal his denial of your motion but the case isn't finalized yet. The appeals court is very unlikely to take an intermediate appeal…Yes I know both sides are facing a great deal of expense…I understand. Yes."

"How much are you prepared to offer?..I see. I'll advise my client. Yes, I'll get back to you."

John hangs up. Everyone looks at him expectantly.

"Well apparently the school board was relying heavily on winning the motion to dismiss and now that they lost they are offering $250,000 to settle the case, but it would require that Steve must voluntarily resign."

Pam asks,

"Do you want me to set up an appointment for Steve to come in and decide if he wants to accept?"

"When I told him about winning the motion the first thing he asked me was if they would give him his job back. Now we know that's not in the deal. But we have to bring him in and explain his chances of winning or losing."

The phone rings. Danny is closest to the phone and answers.

"Offices of John Taylor. He listens, "Hold please, I'll see if he's available."

"This man says he's from the New York Times and he's calling about the judge's decision that holds that there is a God. He wants to talk to you."

"The New York Times. How does that happen so fast?"

Pam comments that apparently all it takes is a little sensationalism.

"I'll talk to him but he'll be disappointed. Hello, this is John Taylor...Yes, I can talk to you about the legal aspects of the case...Yes the case does in one sense include an issue involving whether our earth and the people on it are the product of intelligent design...No it does not mean that the judge ruled that there is a God...You could look at it that way. I suggest you get a transcript of the hearing... Yes that's the court reporter's number. She'll type a transcript for you for a reasonable charge...You're welcome." He hangs up. "Well that's probably the end of that. Now let's set up that meeting with Steve."

Chapter Seventeen

That evening Henry Cobb showed up at the door of Gregg Stryker's home. Greg welcomes him into the living room and they sit facing each other.

"I came as soon as I could Greg. I always want to be careful to avoid being observed meeting with you. I don't want to arouse any suspicion."

"You're right in doing so Henry but I have an important assignment on this Sylvester matter after judge DeLato refused to dismiss the case. My daughter is heavily involved in supporting the school district and she's facing pressure that has her very worried about the school losing. I'd like to know if you can get an influential person on the jury who can guarantee a school board victory."

"I can't guarantee anything but I do know another person who would be willing to play ball. He has a gift for making a good argument and he's a likeable leader type who can most likely swing votes in whatever direction he wants."

"Make sure he knows it will be well worth his time and effort. I want him to be well motivated."

"Don't worry about that. Tell your daughter we can get her a school district victory. Why is it so important to her anyway?"

"She feels threatened by an officer from the national director of her organization who found out that Jill accidentally allowed a confidential internal investigation to get into the hands of Sylvester's attorney."

"That's the report that Taylor tried to get into evidence but the judge wouldn't let him use it so accidental or not it didn't make any difference."

"Apparently that official felt that just the fact that the judge knew of the report influenced his decision so she still blames Jill. Jill came to me quite upset and it's important to me to help her. I want to be sure you understand that and that this potential juror does too. I'll make it worthwhile for both of you."

"I understand that Gregg and I'll make sure my man does."

"Thanks Henry I appreciate that and as always let's keep all this undercover. I was a little concerned about that reporter seeing us together the last time we met."

Chapter Eighteen

It is now the appointment time to reveal the settlement offer to Steve Sylvester. This is a critical time for John. He remembers his last settlement meeting with the plaintiff in the Biggs case. John appreciates how badly Steve wants his job back but he knows how difficult winning Steve's case will be. John would love to settle this case but he knows Steve will be hard to convince he should settle his case without getting his job back. His fear is that he will lose another case where an attractive offer was made and it tears at his gut to think that Steve may lose everything.

John is sitting at his desk. Steve is sitting in front of him. Pam and Danny are working at their desks outside John's office but their real interest is in what is happening in John's office. Pam is worried because she understands how Steve's decision will have an impact on John and doesn't want to see him hurt like the last time on the Bigg's case.

John opens his file and hands the written settlement offer to Steve.

"There it is Steve, $250,000 minus my fee and deposition costs. We have kept costs down since the proponents of ID have been gracious in providing expert witnesses for free."

"What are my chances of winning John?"

"Trying to predict what a jury will do is difficult and unreliable. You know that not one intelligent design case has been won in the federal courts. I know you are teaching only scientific facts but I want you to know that your chances are slim."

"I understand that but they're not offering my job back and with this termination my chances of getting a good paying job are practically nil. I couldn't live for more than 3 or 4 years on the settlement money and the fact that I sued the school board would follow me where ever I went. It might as well be on my résumé, 'Hire me and invite an expensive lawsuit.' No John, I need a job not the money. I'm counting on you to win the case".

"I appreciate your confidence Steve. You know I can't work miracles but I can promise you I'll put everything I have into the case. That's the most I can promise."

"Ok then, let's go for it. And by the way I'm glad you told me to expect a call from the newspaper. First I got a call from the reporter from the local paper. He seemed so excited about this case. Next I got a call from the Associated Press."

"The local reporter's excited because he's trying to make the judge's ruling into a national story. He put it on the news wire and it was picked up by the national media. If the story does get wide media coverage he's got a budding career".

"Why do things have to get so complicated? All I want is my job back and to teach kids to think."

John tries to comfort Steve, saying,

"It seems life isn't simple Steve. And sometimes it puts us into situations we don't expect or want. We get caught up in a web that forces us to react. Situations where we have to decide what's right; situations that test our mettle. Situations that make us decide what we really want in our lives. You've made your choice and for you it's clearly not money and it seems more and more to me that that's the right choice."

Pam has hung up and is letting the phone ring. She happens to look out the window. Her eyes widen and she excitedly runs into John's office.

"Sorry to interrupt John but were getting calls about this case faster than Danny and I can answer and now I see outside there are mobile TV units from all the networks including the cable channels. When I looked they were setting up and they're obviously getting ready to come up here. What do I tell them?"

"Tell anyone who comes up that they'll have to make an appointment if they want to interview me. I'll talk to them but they'll have to decide who gets the first interview. They probably don't know Steve is here. Don't tell them. I'm leading Steve out the back stairs into the garage. I don't think the media would recognize us yet. When they come up tell them I'm not in. I'll call you on your cell."

"Pam, I'm sorry to put you through this. They'll probably act like a pack of wolves. Be calm and professional and we'll work this out together."

John leaves with Steve. This is a panicky and tense situation. The phones are still ringing, adding to the stress of the situation. Pam goes to her phone and mutes it. She tells Danny to do the same. She sits down, goes into her purse, takes out a compact with a mirror, primps her soft brown shoulder length hair, powders her slightly turned up nose, puts on her lipstick, and puts it back into her purse just as five reporters burst into the office. Danny looks busy sitting at his computer.

First reporter, "Are you John's secretary? Is he in? Can we see him?" (Said quickly and excitedly.)

Second reporter, "Has Mr. Taylor issued a statement about the judge's ruling? Could I have your name ma'am?"

Next reporter, "Is Steve Sylvester here? We've been to his house and no one answers the door."

"Please close the door, there are other offices in this building." A reporter closes the door.

"Now, to answer the question my name is Pam Foster. I'm Mr. Taylor's paralegal and office manager. Mr. Taylor is not in."

Reporter: "Where is he? Can we talk to him?"

"Please let me finish. His whereabouts are at the moment are confidential as are Mr. Sylvester's. You will have to make an appointment to interview Mr. Taylor. He's very busy but willing to give an interview. I will make arrangements and it will be on a one and one interview in which Mr. Taylor will explain the case and answer questions. He will not allow Mr. Sylvester to be interviewed without Mr. Taylor himself being present. Now if you will give me your business cards and tell me when you decide who will do the interview and I'll work on setting things up."

The reporters calm down in the face of Pam's professionalism they hand her their business cards, each with a polite 'Thank you and I look forward to working with you Ms. Foster'. As they leave Pam gently closes the door behind them, walks to her desk with calm dignity, then collapses into her chair with great relief and says,

"Whew."

Chapter Nineteen

John arranges for Steve to stay in a motel just out of town, He has a lot on his mind but in view of their recent argument he feels he has to have a serious talk with Jill. He decides that talking to the news media is not a priority and he calls Jill and makes an arrangement to meet at her home that afternoon. Before he arrives Jill and her mother are talking in their living room.

"Jill dear, what is it that John wants to talk to you about that he would come over during his working hours? That's so unlike him."

"Yes it is but he called and said he wanted to talk to me. That it was important."

"Do you think he's finally decided to set a wedding date and he wants to bring you the good news? Oh dear, I hope the August dates haven't been closed at the country club."

"I don't know mother, it doesn't make sense. He's so busy preparing daily for the school board trial it's unlikely that he'd suddenly decide to make wedding plans. He has had so much national attention lately that he may think he's finally achieved prominence as a trial lawyer but I have to tell you that our relationship has been terribly strained lately. He was outraged when he learned that the Women's Alliance for Justice was helping the school board in their case financially. He was even more outraged when he found out that I had the only copy of the school's investigation report and didn't give it to him. We had a big argument over that and I'm not sure he's over it yet."

"Why is this religion business so important to you that you have to argue with him about it?"

"Mother, I learned in college that religion is the opiate of the masses. It prevents logical thinking. People cling to their guns and bibles instead of relying on science and logic. We discuss this all the time at our meetings. We're dedicated to preventing religious teachings and here John is handling a case which would give the schools the right to confuse students' minds on the subject. It's entirely contrary to what our Alliance believes in. I told that to John when we last met and we argued about it. He feels that people should be free to decide for themselves and I feel that propagandizing young vulnerable minds with religion interferes with their right thinking in later years."

"Is this issue something that could lead to a breakup?"

"John thinks of himself as a strong willed man but I know his upbringing. He rates himself by his achievements. If he were to win this case it would bolster his will and he would never give in to me. But he's in for a surprise because he's not going to win."

"How can you be so sure?"

"Mother you haven't had many confidential discussions with father lately have you?

"Dear I don't know what you're talking about. Anyway isn't it possible he's fatigued and simply wants some feminine companionship?"

"It seems to me that he gets all he needs from that secretary of his. He's spending a lot of money on experts and depositions and she's agreed to reduce her salary until the trial is over. That sounds like a lot more than a mere secretary would do for her boss. If we get married I'm going to insist that he fire her."

"As your father says, 'show no mercy to the competition'. Well I hear a car in the driveway. I'll get out of here and leave you two alone."

She leaves, Jill opens the door for John and immediately sees from the look on his face that something is wrong. By her greeting it's apparent that she's ready for a battle.

"Hello John, you look concerned about something. Has your case taken a turn for the worse?"

"That's what I came to talk about. We last argued about this case when I found out that you had a copy of the school's investigation report and you gave it to Creighton Harding and not me."

"Don't bring that up again. I told you that my organization received that report in confidence and I couldn't give it out to just anyone."

"But you gave it to my opponent without any misgivings."

"There's no breach of confidentially there because he represents the school."

"You could have made him subpoena it and then I would have learned about it while discovery was still open. Look, it seems that you are more interested in helping the school board rather than me. I represent this man because I think he's right in what he's trying to do. You apparently have this belief that young people's minds must be programmed to a secular scientific ideal that worships intellectuals and their theories. And let me tell you that what I've seen from some of these elites, their egos interfere with their judgment."

"You say you're representing him because he's right. That sounds so noble. Yet as long as I've known you you've talked about being a great trial lawyer and getting big verdicts. This case makes you look like a money grubbing lawyer."

John is stunned and his first reaction is to convince her that he's not doing this just for money.

"I told you all I wanted was for Steve to get his job back with the right to teach as he sees fit."

"But this case involves a claim for money damages. Don't deny it."

"I had to fashion this case so the school has more to lose other than a simple job reinstatement otherwise they'd be willing to try the case with little or nothing to lose. You know that."

Jill, getting angry, continues,

"We've talked about this over and over. You can't seem to see my side of it. I have reasons for what I'm doing."

"This has something to do with your position at the Woman's Alliance for Justice doesn't it?

"What right do you have to ask me about my relationship with my club?"

"What right do you have to tell me how to run my business? Why is it that your precious club is so opposed to generally accepted facts being presented in a science class?"

"We're opposed to teaching fairy tales to students and if you weren't so interested in making money you'd see it that way too."

"So there it is. You and your club are so intent on preventing religion from being considered as an option that you are willing to erect a firewall against any factual information that may validly illustrate a fallacy in your dogmatic theories and you blindly insist that my motives are purely monetary rather than trying to simply allow a fair presentation for both sides of the question. How can you consider marrying me when you look at me as a money grubbing shyster?"

John is totally angry now, his face is red and he is standing face to face. Jill replies sarcastically,

"Well darling, you make a good looking trophy husband."

To John, the realization that he was nothing more to Jill than an object to display, was the final confirmation of the suspicion he had that this family used people to fit into their goals; which was the very reason he insisted on developing his own independence. This was all he needed to decide that his commitment to marry into the family was a terrible mistake. The time had come to put an end to it.

"Well you've certainly learned well from your father. Well maybe this isn't in this scheme of yours but you can kiss our engagement goodbye."

"I thought you might say that. Here's your ring back, you'll probably need it to finance your case. Goodbye and just for your information Creighton Harding is single and has asked me out to dinner. Nothing to do with the case of case of course. I assume you can find the door."

Jill walks into the next room, leaving John standing there. He stands there for a moment then says loudly so she can hear,

"If he weren't my opponent I'd warn him".

Chapter Twenty

The next morning Pam arrives early at the office. It is still dark and Pam is unlocking the door to open for the day. She enters in, turns on the lights, puts her purse in her desk drawer and sits down at her desk. She turns her computer on and as it warms up she speaks her innermost feelings that morning although there is no one there to hear. She is not aware that John has ended his engagement with Jill.

"Good morning computer, what have you in store for me today? A note from John? Let's see what the latest is from a man engaged to be married to the wrong woman."

John has left a hand written note and a tape on her desk.

She reads John's message,

"Pam, I'm leaving the office early because I've got some matters to clear up with Jill."

Then, expressing her own feelings she says,

"That woman doesn't know how lucky she is to be engaged to you John. I pray that she would understand that and treat you with the respect you deserve".

She continues reading speaking as she reads,

"I've got to redo my trial brief. I don't think the one I've done is right. I've got to take the time to put my heart into it."

Pam speaks her thoughts out loud again,

"John, if you only knew how I put my heart into everything I do for you, and how I longed that you would put me into your heart. And how difficult it has been for me to be near you since you announced your engagement. But if you feel that it's the right thing for you then I guess God has something else planned for me. It hurts but I know things happen that way."

Pam goes back to reading John's message,

"I'll finish it tonight, probably late. I'll drop by the office and put the tape on your desk. I'd appreciate it if you could give this priority so I can proof read it and make any necessary changes. Thanks."

"You've still got my priority John. Ok, so let's get to work."

Pam puts on earphones, places a tape in a dictation machine, sets up the computer and begins to type.

Chapter Twenty One

At the same time that morning Judge DeLato is in his office talking to Detective Tom Ryan from the local police department. The judge speaks,

"I've read your investigation report Detective Ryan. Tell me how this all came about."

"I'm sorry to spring this on you so suddenly judge but I was waiting for an opportunity to talk to you when Henry took a day off. This investigation has to be completely confidential. You've read my report on what information we have to date. It appears that your clerk has been manipulating the jury pool and putting people in who are willing to make the verdict go the way he directs. We were put on to this by Chris Ott, the reporter. He covered the Bigg's trial and tried to interview the jurors. One of them finally called him and was upset by the way the jury foreman disregarded your instructions and put an undue amount of pressure on the other jurors to find that the defendants did nothing wrong. This led us to an interview with that foreman who eventually broke down after questioning and confessed that Henry paid him to influence the verdict. He doesn't know where the money was coming from other than he thinks there was someone with big bucks financing the deal."

"Any idea how long this may have been going on?"

"Not at this point but that's why I'm here judge. I want permission to wiretap Henry's phone to see if we can catch him red handed if he's trying to do this again. In the meantime we don't want any hint of this investigation getting out. We don't want anything to change so that Henry might become suspicious."

"That's fine Tom. I'll cooperate with you in every way. Keep me advised how the investigation is going."

"I will judge. I've prepared an order allowing a phone tap for your signature which I obviously don't want to go through routine channels."

"Fine." He signs the order.

"Thanks judge, goodbye."

"Goodbye."

Chapter Twenty Two

That same morning John, who had been working all night and into the morning on his trial brief, slept late and takes a break from trial preparation to have lunch with Frank at the Bench and Bar. They sit at a table across from the bar. The tables are covered with red and white checkered table cloths with large bowls of peanuts. The floor is oak wood planking with peanut shells on the floor around the tables. The atmosphere is friendly and relaxed.

The waitress has taken their order and brought each a 16 ounce draft. Frank is asking about the progress of John's case and as they talk the noon news is on the large screen television set. The media are still focusing on what they call the "monkey trial", comparing it to the famous Scope trial in the 1920's where a teacher was put on trial for teaching evolution. The story interrupts their conversation as they watch. The announcer does the lead in,

"We've been following the Sylvester v. Montgomery School Board case in Hilltown, Indiana where our local reporter Daryl Corbett tells us of some new developments."

"That's right Carl. We learned today that there were settlement talks between the attorneys in the case but the parties could not reach an agreement on terms so that means that the case will proceed to trial. The school board claims Mr. Sylvester is teaching intelligent design. There have been several cases involving intelligent design in the federal courts and those cases have more or less routinely held that ID was a religious doctrine but judge DeLato created an uproar when he decided that there were sufficient facts to allow the case to go to a jury. Since then some media reports have sensationalized their coverage by claiming that the jury will be deciding if there is a God. That's not quite accurate because this is in essence a wrongful termination case but there is that religious element involved which makes it interesting."

"Do we know what the terms of the settlement were Daryl?"

"Those terms were confidential but it has been rumored that Mr. Sylvester wanted his job back and that's not part of the offer."

"Alright Daryl. We'll continue to follow your reports with interest. In other news today..."

Resuming their conversation, Frank says,

"It sounds as though the reporter came close to getting it right. John every time I hear the term 'intelligent design', it brings to my mind that by definition it assumes a superior being."

"So is that a valid reason for not teaching the complexity of biological systems which common sense and even mathematical calculations show are essentially impossible to have occurred by chance?"

"Are there any explanations from the other side as to how evolution occurred?"

"All of their explanations are couched in terms of 'that could be' or 'this could have been possible.' But unless you can demonstrate or prove them, there's no basis for shutting off other possibilities. They offer simple explanations how somethings could start to develop without taking into considering the total of the tens to hundreds of steps that have to occur for a completed organ to work. Most organs are tremendously complex with parts so small and so precisely created that we don't have the machines to make them ourselves. Yet we attribute that miracle to chance."

"Well you got past one obstacle with the judge, do you think you'll be able to convince a jury?"

"That's the big question Frank. You know no one can predict what a jury will do."

"I will say that you've really got into his case John. It's almost as if you want to prove something to yourself. Are you becoming religious?"

John responds sarcastically,

"Oh heaven forbid that that should happen. No, I'm being facetious. But I am keeping an open mind myself. How can I convince anyone to keep an open mind if I don't have a like mind?"

"Is this the same lawyer I knew that had his life all lined up for success? To try to win a million dollar verdict? To marry well and go onward and upward up the ladder of success?"

"I am changing. I've seen what seems to go along with that type of so called success and I didn't like what I saw."

"Frank, I'm going to tell you something and I ask that you keep it totally to yourself. Last night I went to Jill's house to discuss her devoting all her efforts to helping my opponent. The discussion got ugly and it finally became obvious that Jill had all of her father's characteristics, particularly in using people to accomplish their goals. In the heat of the argument she admitted that the only thing I meant to her was as a trophy to parade around before her elitist friends. That was why there was so much opposition to my having an independent business. It kept them from using me as a political tool. I'm now certain that Jill's father wanted me as a district attorney so he could get away with some shady business deal he has planned. Being called a puppet dancing on strings was enough for me and I called the engagement off. But I don't want that known and have some gossip society page reporter pestering me while I'm involved in this trial. So please Frank, don't tell anyone."

"Your secrets safe with me buddy but are you going to tell Pam? I haven't said anything but I think I've seen something in the way looks at you that tells me she should know this."

"Do you really think so Frank? I'm afraid I'm helpless when it comes to seeing things like that"

"I think you should tell her John. She's so loyal to you and she's smart. Not only that, she is beautiful with a killer body."

"I will tell her. You know Frank my life has just turned around by 180 degrees and I suppose I should be stunned but with all of the changes. I just have the feeling I'm doing the right thing and I feel good about it."

Frank says philosophically,

"You know that we started law school with great ideas about changing the world. We thought we'd be knights in shining armor, fighting injustice and enabling justice for all. Then we got into the system and found that it wasn't as easy as we thought. It was easier to go along to get along. It pays off financially but sometimes things happen that make you feel that you need a shower. Now you've got a true quest and it makes you feel the way you did when you decided to become a lawyer… and from what I'm seeing in you it's a healthy feeling."

"You're right, John pauses, but frankly Frank, We better stop slobbering in our beer."

"Right. It makes us too emotional for guys. Next thing we'll be talking about relationships."

John, straightening up and feigning a macho attitude, clearing his throat and in a deep voice says,

"Can't have that. How'd you like that Colts victory last Sunday?"

Frank, assuming the same posture,

"They killed 'em. Nothing like a lot of good heavy bodily contact to make a great game."

John, continuing,

"Even a little blood thrown in for good measure."

"You're a manly guy John."

"So are you Frank. But maybe we better leave before we have to beat someone up in here."

They stand up, toss down their beers and walk toward the exit door patting each other on the back and laughing.

Chapter Twenty Three

Later in the day, just before closing, John and Pam are in the office putting together the finishing touches for the trial. Pam says,

"I've finished the trial brief and here it is. It sounds really good. I think it's the best you've ever done"

John, who couldn't think of the best way to tell Pam, finally just blurted it out,

"Thanks Pam. I have to tell you, yesterday I left the office early and had a showdown with Jill. She was working against me on this case the whole time. She has an entirely different outlook on life than I do. I'm glad I figured that out in time so now the engagement is off. (At this point Pam who is standing, reacts visibly. Her knees weaken and she leans on her desk.)

"Are you all right?"

"Oh, yes I just lost my balance for a minute"

"Anyway I felt so much better about the whole thing that I went home and rewrote the brief. I thought I had it done a week ago but that version didn't seem right. I totally revised it and once I got into it I couldn't stop. I stayed up late into the night to finish it and then went to the office to drop it off and went to bed and slept like a baby. That's why I'm late today."

"John you've never worked as hard on any case we've had before. What is it that you find so fascinating?

"I'm not sure. Maybe it's the subject matter. I've never been involved in such a deep subject. This case crosses back and forth of the border between philosophy and science with the deepest questions regarding both the beginning and the meaning of life. Something that I've never considered before and now I realize I should have. Everyone should."

He looks at Pam who is looking at him with admiration.

"Pam we have been through a lot together and I've been grateful for your sticking with me particularly on this case where you've worked as hard as I have. I want you to know that I rely on you for your skills and encouragement and more than that, I'm realizing that I don't know what I would do without you."

Pam, putts her hand on his and John responds by moving closer, looking into her eyes.

"John, I've enjoyed every minute we've been together. Your zeal has infected me. But John you don't know how it makes me feel to hear you say that."

John, taking both her hands and looking straight in her eyes.

"I was hoping it would. That's why I said it. I can't believe what a fool I've been. I was looking for the wrong thing when all along I had the right thing, you, right before my eyes"

"John, I feel the same way about you."

John moves close to Pam, looking intently into her eyes. Pam, even though she wanted him to advance says,

"John, we've got to concentrate on the job at hand for now."

John, reluctantly, gets back to business.

"Right now I'd like to forget about the trial but you're right as always. OK, we've got the witnesses lined up. We got a real break when we were provided with expert witnesses who volunteered to testify. I want to get respected experts on first so the jury doesn't think that Steve is some kind of crackpot. Then I'll put Steve on the stand to echo the expert testimony and to testify that he's supporting free and open thinking and not a religion. That should be enough to get us past a directed verdict but then the real issue will come when the defense puts on Dr. Adler who is a skilled powerful witness. He acts very knowledgeable and lectures like a professor. I've got to stop him from establishing a rapport with the jury. If I can't I'm afraid we can't win."

"I'm sure you have it all together so why not get some rest since you hardly slept at all last night and I'll see you early in the morning."

"You're right Pam, and I can't wait. I'll see you then."

John remembers her statement about not moving too fast but before he leaves he puts his hand to his lips and throws her a kiss, looking at her with a smile as he does, then turns and leaves.

Pam spends a few moments closing things up in the office, then looks up to heaven and says,

"Thank you Lord".

She walks out and locks the door.

Chapter Twenty Four

Three weeks have passed and the trial has been proceeding. John and Pam have been working many evenings together, restraining themselves while growing deeper in love. John's witnesses were at the top of their field, consisting of two experts in micro biology and a respected astronomer/physicist. As expected the micro biologists testified of the complexity of the human body and the impossibility of some critical organs coming into completion without its components having yet developed. The astronomer/physicist explained how science proved that the universe exploded into existence from nothing, that prior thereto there was no matter. A fourth witness, a mathematician, testified that the odds against the universe exploding into existence by chance are so enormous that by admitted scientific standards, it is impossible. All clearly testified that no scientist could explain how the universe came into existence from nothing and that no scientist could explain how life began.

In contrast, Creighton's witness demonstrated, through the use of photographs on a screen, the supposed progression of humanoid skeleton remains from ancient times through the ages. It was difficult for the jury to see the changes demonstrated by the expert paleontologist but his words were said with such certainty that the jury could simply believe him without really understanding. Other defense biologists testified the manner in which complex organs developed was in small progressive steps. They cited fossil evidence that they claimed showed the progressive development that could have eventually become modern skeleton sections. Although there was no direct evidence to prove it.

The testimony was evenly balanced until Creighton put his primary witness on the stand. Dr. Adler is a smooth and confident witness with excellent credentials. Upon questioning by Creighton he is very positive in extolling the validity of evolution, and quite convincing. Creighton's last question to Dr. Adler is,

"So Dr. Adler, in light of your testimony will you tell the jury if, in your opinion, there is any scientific validity to intelligent design?"

"No, I think it is entirely unscientific and harmful to the minds of young students."

Creighton says,

"Your witness counselor."

Many observers think that Dr. Adler's testimony shifted the balance of opinion very much in favor of the school district. John must convince the jury that his evidence is more convincing than Creighton's. From the way the evidence stood as Dr. Adler finished his answers to Creighton's questions, it was apparent that John was going to lose unless he could show, by cross examining Dr. Adler, that his testimony was false. So as John's turn came up to cross examine, he knew it was his last chance to win and everything depended on his skill in getting this witness to admit to the fallacies of evolution. On that the case will stand or fall.

Chapter Twenty Five

The court room is silent and all eyes are on John as he rises and walks toward Dr. Adler. The judge is on the bench. The jury is in the jury box. All of the partitions separating the parties are modern, done in blond oak as are the tables for the attorneys and the benches for the observers. Steve is sitting in the front row of the observer's seats. Danny and Pam are there also.

The court reporter is on the side next to the witness stand. The court officer sits off to the other side of the judge and Dr. Adler is sitting in the witness stand looking smug. John begins his cross examination,

"Dr. Adler, there's been a great deal of discussion about facts in this case and you have heard testimony that the theory of evolution is being taught as a fact. Do you believe that it should be taught as a fact sir?"

"I think it is reasonable to do so, yes."

"The dictionary defines a fact as a truth known by actual experience or observation. Do you agree with that definition?"

"I would agree with the term 'a truth known by observation'. I believe that the changes we see in fossils allow us to make that conclusion."

"By fossils you mean skulls and bones buried way back in time which are dug up and observed'"

"That's correct."

"Dr. Adler, I show you this exhibit which is an illustration contained in many high school biology texts which show an artist's conception of an ape gradually morphing into a human. Do you recognize this as an exhibit used in high school?"

"Yes it's an artist's conception as to how the human developed."

"Am I correct that no person has observed this to occur?"

"Of course not. This is something that occurred over eons of time. No human alive has observed this".

"Dr. Adler, what does the term 'missing link' refer to in paleontology?"

"That's a term that describes the unfortunate fact that although we hypothesize how man and apes had a common ancestor, we have not yet found the intermediate link that would prove the concept."

When John makes a point for the jury, he looks at the jury which emphasizes that point.

"You said hypothesize. That means the theory is hypothetical. No one has discovered the gradual or intermediate step, the missing link, that proves the theory?"

"True, but it is thought that in time it will be found."

You say in time. To say that evolution is a fact without the missing link, isn't that counting your chickens before they're hatched? "

"A great majority of scientists stand behind this theory."

"Have there been instances where a great majority of scientists have stood behind theories which ultimately were proved to be wrong?"

"Yes indeed that's true but it doesn't mean that Darwin's theory is wrong this time."

"But my point is that your assertion about the great majority doesn't prove that his theory is correct now does it?"

"My opinion is that the majority agrees because our observations support the theory."

"But isn't it presumptive to teach evolution as a fact and to show an illustration of an artist's conception when in fact the critical proof has never been found?"

"We must teach our students to think logically and scientifically and not be confused by myths and fairy tales such as proposed by the theories of your witnesses."

"You say think logically but I don't suppose that you would concede that teaching something as a fact when it is unproven is propaganda rather than logic?"

Creighton stands, "Objection your honor, he's arguing with the witness."

"Withdraw the question your honor. Let's get back to the beginning doctor. What did Darwin have to say about how life began?"

"Darwin proposed that in the early earth there may have been chemicals present in a warm pool to form amino acids which are the building blocks of life. He believed it happened by chance."

"And how much did Darwin know about the complexity of a cell and the DNA molecule at that time?"

"At that time a cell was thought to be a simple organism and he had no idea of DNA or the enormous complexity of even the simplest cell which we have observed with the electron microscope. Scientists are no longer certain that life happened by chance. Various theories are proposed but none has been officially accepted.

"You say scientists no longer are certain that life happened by chance because of what they observe by using the electron microscope, which is many times more powerful than the optical, to observe a cell?"

"It is. No such extremely powerful equipment was available then to Darwin."

"Can you describe what is known about the construction of a cell doctor?"

"It's far too complicated to describe in detail but I'll describe it in the simplest terms possible. For life to continue the cell must be able to reproduce itself. The construction of a new cell is controlled by information contained in the DNA molecule which gives instructions on how chemicals are combined to form protein. The DNA opens to allow what we call a messenger to pick up and carry information to other chemical machines which must in turn allow certain of the chemical units to combine to form the necessary proteins. This process is in itself extremely complicated since these molecules must fold in order to give the proper instructions. When they do a protein is formed. This is a very simplified description."

"You mean it's even more complicated than what you've described?"

"Much more so. These events must not only follow the correct instructions and each event must occur in the proper sequence."

"You've told us that the DNA molecule is necessary to create protein."

"That is true."

"And is it true that protein is a necessary component of DNA?"

"Yes"

"Then, at the beginning of life, how could protein be constructed before there was DNA or how could DNA exist before there was protein?"

"We're not certain of that. Some have their theories."

"Doesn't that lead to the conclusion that they were both part of a concurrent design?"

"From a scientific standpoint I can only say that how it happened is not certain at this time?"

"Excuse me for saying so doctor but your answer is akin to burying your head in the sand. You've already told us that the formation of organic molecules from inorganic minerals can't be explained and now we have an even greater mystery. We have a DNA molecule with all those enormous internal coded directions on how to build a protein and yet the DNA molecule itself is constructed of protein before there are any instructions on how to build protein. If protein popped into existence first where did it get the information to build a DNA molecule? And the same can be said about DNA, where did the information come from to build something as complicated as a protein?"

Dr. Adler does not want to admit that science is completely ignorant of the most basic concepts of creation. And he hates to have to say it over again. He responds in a haughty manner,

"I've already said that can't be explained with certainty."

"But can't we come to a logical conclusion from what we do know? We know that life, from your perspective animals, phyla, came into existence equipped with all the necessary information to duplicate themselves. We know they had to have information that may be equivalent to a ten thousand page encyclopedia don't we doctor?"

"It is logical that a first life event contained all the necessary information for chemical machinery to reproduce itself otherwise life would not have continued."

"I'll take that as a yes. You have described to us how complicated cell reproduction is. Isn't it true that even the most basic form of animal life had to have the DNA and the proteins and all of the instructions and information that go along with it in order to duplicate itself?"

Dr. Adler, after a pause and some internal struggling, responds,

"I will admit that?"

John looks at the jury to emphasize the important admission he needed to develop his strategy, then says,

"Thank you for that doctor. And now I have the ultimate question, where did this information come from?"

Dr. Adler, again forced to admit the ignorance of the so called 'know-it all' body of science, grudgingly says,

"If scientists can't answer your original question about the beginning of life they cannot answer that question counsel."

"There is no dispute that information contained in DNA is intelligence is there doctor?"

"The information you refer to is intelligence."

"I'm certain you know of Richard Dawkins, the renowned critic of intelligent design, yet even he admits that life has the appearance of design. The dictionary defines design as the adaption of a means or plan to a preconceived end. Do you agree that the biological system of cell duplication has the appearance of a means or plan to a preconceived end?"

"I have already said that it is a very complicated procedure which does achieve cell duplication. You use the term preconceived which presumes a pre-existing intelligence. I'm afraid I can't agree with that concept."

"And that is because scientists can't accept anything but a natural materialistic cause isn't it?"

"Yes. Scientists can't believe in supernatural beings. First life was an amazing event. We can't explain it. As far as we're concerned it was a one-time unexplained phenomenon so we'll leave it there until we can prove what happened and go on to studying how life evolved from there on."

"You say 'leave it there'. So are you saying that science demands that no one dare even think

about the beginning of life?

"No, I'm not saying that."

"And well you should not because even now scientists are searching for the beginning of life, but have no answers and cannot create life itself. Isn't that true?"

"It is true that all of the various theories are speculation and none of them can create life".[1]

"As a matter of fact Dr. Hawking, the brilliant cosmologist, has propounded the idea that life was created by an abundance of 'life seeds' spread throughout the universe. He has received no criticism or ridicule for propounding that theory has he?'

"That theory is known as panspermia and it has been respected as a theory only."

"Is there any evidence to support the theory?"

"It has not been considered as any more than speculation."[2]

"Is there any mention as to who created the seeds?"

"The theory can only assume that somehow organic material formed in outer space or there are superior beings who are eons ahead of us in intelligence who created organic material, or seeds of life if you will."

Well if organic material formed by chance that doesn't explain where the intelligence came from to produce life, only intelligent beings would explain organized intelligent information, true?"

"I have already said that there is intelligent information in DNA".

"Which means there had to be a source for the intelligence, true?"

Dr. Adler cannot deny that there must be a source for information.

"There must be a source for information whether it be trial and error or implanted."

John has just established another critical point in his cross examination strategy.

"Thank you for that doctor Adler." (And the doctor wonders why he is being thanked.)

"Now you've previously testified that you cannot accept that life was a preconceived plan because the term 'preconceived' indicates an existing intelligence and you couldn't accept that concept"

"Yes?"

"Don't you see the inconsistency in your testimony by saying on the one hand that you can't accept the idea of a superior intelligence yet when it comes to panspermia science does accept without criticism the possible concept of a superior intelligence?"

"Dr. Adler is flummoxed. He realizes he's made an error in what is supposed to be faultless testimony.

Dr. Adler stammers:

"It-It's different, it's not- not the same thing."

"How is it different if one of the bases for panspermia theorizes that an intelligent being created life?"

"But panspermia doesn't imply that a deity did it."

"Neither does intelligent design. It merely proves that life contains intelligence which could not have happened by chance. Which is a tacit admission scientists make when they propose that some superior alien being did it. Doctor, you will find no intelligent design publications or literature which claims that a deity created life. If such information were available you can be certain defense counsel would have produced it as evidence in this case. And he has not done so. So where is the difference between panspermia and intelligent design?"

Dr. Adler hesitates and says nothing for a very long pause, such a pause that it becomes uncomfortable for him and his lawyer. He finally says,

"I cannot answer that question."

"You're admitting, doctor, that there is no difference. You cannot say that there is a difference."

"I'm saying I cannot answer that question."

"The question is 'what is the difference' and you can't answer that question. In effect you are saying that you cannot describe any difference. Anyone using common sense would accept that means there is no difference. Now if there's no difference what right does the school board have to allow the teaching of panspermia but not intelligent design?"

"I'm not a lawyer Mr. Taylor, so that's not a question for me to answer.

"I'll withdraw the question sir, I think the answer is obvious."

Creighton who has seen the witness being destroyed before his very eyes finally has something to object to,

"Objection your honor, counsel is commenting on the evidence. This isn't closing argument."

"I'm simply saying that the answer is obvious your honor."

"That will be up to the jury to decide counsel. Objection sustained."

"I apologize your honor I've withdrawn the question." Nevertheless, John feels he has made his point with the jury.

"Getting back to the phenomenon of first life doctor, Will you also accept that the same type of phenomenon resulted in an enormous number of new animals of different species which came into existence in a relatively short period of time without any previous ancestor from which they could have evolved?"

"I assume you are referring to the Cambrian Period when a plethora of new animals appeared in a relatively short period of time."

"That's exactly what I'm referring to and as you admit it was a time when many, many new species came into existence without an ancestor just as the first animal did. If you were to count the whole period of time that the earth existed as 24 hours, the time period in which these animals occurred would be just one minute.[3] That is completely contrary to Darwin's theory isn't it? Because evolution, according to Darwin, requires eons of time to develop slowly one minor step at a time?"

"It is."

"They were brand new animals which were enormously more complex with new organs, new digestive systems, bowel and waste disposal systems all completely developed without ancestors to explain their development; all in an extremely short period in evolutional time, isn't that true doctor?"

"That is true. There have been various attempts to find clear evidence of ancestors but these attempts have not been generally accepted."

"Darwin himself said that if there were unexplained animal developments without a lengthy enough period of time for such developments to occur gradually then his theory would be wrong didn't he? And he was aware of and specifically referring to the animals in the Cambrian period."

"He did say that."

John looks at the jury to emphasize the point.

"So we have Darwin himself saying that if certain events occurred his theory would be wrong plus the fact that such events did occur. In other words, Shouldn't that be enough in itself to refute the theory of evolution?"

"Scientists have learned a great deal since Darwin's time counsel. We now believe that mutated genes are passed on to the next generation and that is how new species of animals develop."

"You are avoiding my question doctor. There were no ancestors at all. The mutation you refer to would have to be in the DNA of an ancestor and transmitted to the new animal. The Cambrian animals had no ancestor?"

"Mutation cannot exist if there is no ancestor that is true. I am not ready to admit that they had no ancestor. I believe an ancestor will be found."

"Dr. Adler, you know that scientists have been desperately searching for an ancestor ever since Darwin's time. You are a scientist, do you have any accepted peer reviewed scientific evidence that establishes with reasonable certainty that there were ancestors for the Cambrian animals?"

"I do not."

"Then can you deny that with all available peer reviewed information the Cambrian explosion of new animals occurred in the same manner as the first life event with no ancestor to pass on genetic information and no known method for the origin of the information?"

"If you assume there are no ancestors then that would be the conclusion."

"Thank you for that Dr. Adler. Now let me move on to another subject.

Dr. Adler, his ego bruised by John's cross exam, now is of a mind to cooperate with John as far as is possible without giving everything away. He hopes his cooperation will tone down John's future questioning. In addition to that he enjoys lecturing laymen as if he were a professor in college.

"Is it true that the universe did not exist forever but had a beginning?"

"That is true. It was always thought that the universe had been in existence forever until Dr. Hubble discovered that the frequency of light changed as the universe expands. This phenomenon is known as the Doppler affect and is indicative that the universe is expanding. It's that the frequency of light lowers as the stars move away from us much as the sound of a train whistle lowers its frequency as a train passes us and moves away. This was consistent with Einstein's theory of relativity and the expansion of the universe has been consistent with other known factors such that it is now considered an accepted fact. Not only that, the universe continues to expand currently which means that in the past it was increasingly smaller and smaller until eons in the past it was nothing."

"Are you saying that the universe began from nothing?"

"Yes, if it is getting bigger as time passes then as one goes back in time it was ultimately smaller until it was nothing. Not only am I saying it but the most respected cosmologists and physicists are saying it. The universe was created from nothing counsel, in an instant. Before that there was nothing, no time, no space, **No matter**.[4] The universe with all its laws exploded into existence along with space, time and matter.

"Is it known how this happened or how it was caused doctor? Can there be anything that begins to exist without a cause?"

"It is unknown how this occurred. How all this happened when nothing existed before the universe is a total mystery."

"Isn't it true that the design of the universe exhibits intelligence through the universal constants doctor?"

"There are approximately 20 factors that are constant throughout the universe. You could call them rules such as the speed of light, the force of gravity, the force that holds atoms together and so on. The fact that they are so finely tuned to support life gives the appearance of design. For instance the force of gravity is finely tuned to twelve digits beyond the decimal point. All of the constants are finely tuned. For any one of them to be different by a decimal point or two would make life on earth impossible.

"Isn't it likely then that such a finely tuned universe had to be designed by an intelligence? Isn't it considered impossible for all these variables to be so precisely set without intelligence as a guide?"[5]

"It is scientifically classified as impossible but fortunately there is a scientific explanation as to how this could have occurred."

"Really, please tell us how this finely tuned miracle which is against impossible odds can be explained other than by intelligence."

"Although the probabilities are impossible against our universe being so precisely formed by chance to allow humans to exist, the matter can be explained if there were a constant explosion of new universes, each with a different set of constants until our universe happened by chance."

John, looking at the jury in amazement, replies,

"Really doctor? First it was aliens from outer space and now it is alien universes? Is there some unpublished evidence of millions, perhaps trillions of alien universes? What evidence is there doctor? "

"Well, it is felt that it is the only possible explanation."

"It is the only possible explanation if you are compelled to believe in a mindless materialistic universe on which evolution is based. This mindless materialistic view is contrary to known events such as the universe popping into existence perfectly designed for human life, the first life popping into existence with all of the encyclopedic information contained in the DNA, the explosion of new animals in the Cambrian period with no ancestor who could have provided the information for the development of the all the new organs which had never previously existed. Is it so hard to conclude that if such events are known to happen, each of them just reeking with created intelligence; that intelligence is the overriding factor in all that begins to exist?"

"What would you have me say? That's it's easy to explain, that we can easily conclude that whenever something we don't understand happens that it's some miraculous intervention and say it explains everything. This is what is known as the god of the gaps theory. Just imagine where science would be over the centuries if scientists had relied on a god of the gaps theory to explain every phenomenon. We would still be in the dark ages."

"You raise a false argument. Which of the great scientists in the past centuries has given up on research concerning an unknown phenomenon because of religion, Newton on physics, Lavoisier on chemistry, Planck's work on atomic and sub-atomic processes and on and on? These men were giants in their respective fields. Whom can you name who gave up research because of religion?"

John pauses to give Dr. Adler a moment to think. He is silent.

"You can't name one. The god of the gaps theory explains what is not known by saying God does it. Neither current scientific theory nor intelligent design make that claim."

"But intelligent design cites intelligence which implies there is a god. That is the difference."

"So also do the scientists who propose panspermia. They claim a superior intelligence created life on earth, No one prohibits their theory even though they are the same in their claim that intelligence is the basic factor in the creation of life."

"But ID uses the word 'intelligence' which implies a conscious mind. Darwinism does no such thing. It is based on a totally mindless, materialistic premise."

"But panspermia claims intelligent alien beings created life and the theory is not condemned. Are you saying the main difference is that they use a fancy word to describe the theory?

"Perhaps intelligent design should be known as the origin of man without a known cause."

"Perhaps Darwinism should be known as a mindless theory of the beginning of man."

Creighton has an opportunity to object again,

"Objection your honor, counsel is testifying. That's not a question.

"I'm merely responding to the witnesses' comment your honor

Judge DeLato responds,

"Let's keep moving along gentlemen."

"Doctor Adler, without regard as to what we call intelligent design, it is true is it not, that the panspermia theory is supported by renowned scientists in their field? This theory is propounded by some of the most respected cosmologists in the field such as Stephen Hawking, Fred Hoyle, and Francis Crick who discovered DNA, all of whom are atheists. Is that correct?"

"That is correct."

"And with regard to these seeds, they contained the information to create the first animal with the ability to reproduce? And further that information is intelligence, correct? So according to the theory some alien intelligence implanted that intelligence?"

"That is true according to that theory."

"So there are some of the most respected scientists who theorize that there are beings who have intelligence far superior to mankind who developed and distributed the seeds for life but are not gods. You certainly must admit that following what you have just said?"[6]

Again after a short pause and realizing such an admission must follow from what he has just said he responds,

"I admit that some scientists believe that."

"So there are respected scientists who publish peer reviewed articles which propose that intelligent beings designed the plan of life. That is the same thing that intelligent design proponents are saying except those scientists attribute the design to aliens and intelligent design makes no conclusion as to the author of that intelligence. So why shouldn't ID be allowed to be taught as an alternate theory? By the way, whom do panspermia theorists claim created the aliens?"

Dr. Adler has to save face here somehow. He knows that there are respected scientists who believe that life was begun by aliens. He decides the best he can do is give up something to get something.

"I will admit it has that right if you will admit that intelligent design does not claim or attempt to prove a deity."

At this point Creighton, who has his elbows resting on the counsel's table, drops his head into his hands.

"I thank you very much for your candor doctor. I had many more questions I intended to ask you but based on your answers I rest my case because intelligent design does not intend to prove there is a deity. The purpose of this case is to prove that ID has the same right to be taught side by side with Darwinism and that the board discharged Mr. Sylvester wrongfully. Now that you have admitted that there's no need to continue."

There is a rumble of muted comments in the court room from spectators and the reporters watching the trial. No one expected the trial to end so abruptly but from John's point of view he has proven his case because the defense's prime witness has admitted that Steve Sylvester had a right to teach as he was and therefore he was wrongfully discharged. Judge DeLato immediately takes charge and says,

"We will recess at this time to discuss motions. The jury is excused. I instruct you once again not to discuss this testimony you have heard until I give you instructions."

The clerk asks all to stand while, the jury files out and the judge leaves the bench. As soon as the judge leaves the court room erupts into loud talk about John's cross exam, how unexpectedly short it was, how Dr. Adler admitted that respected scientists demonstrate that there can be intelligent information implanted in new life without the necessity of a deity. That is the same position of intelligent design. So the defense has failed to prove that intelligent design promotes religion and that there was no good cause to fire Steve Sylvester.

Chapter Twenty Six

It is a few hours later and both counsel have learned that Judge DeLato is still very interested in moving this trial along quickly. While the jury was absent the attorneys could make their motions. The judge denied Creighton's motion for a new trial because there was no valid basis for the motion. John made no motions since he was satisfied with the trial procedure. Ordinarily the court would have allowed more time for the attorneys to prepare for their closing arguments but he had previously warned the attorneys to have their arguments prepared in advance. The jury was now called back to hear closing arguments and the judge says,

"Are you ready to give your closing argument Mr. Taylor?"

"I am your honor." He stands and addresses the jury.

"Members of the jury. I want to emphasize the basic points that are critical in this case. First of all the purpose of this trial, the underlying critical issue, is not whether or not there is a God. The critical issue is whether the school board had a legal right to fire Steve Sylvester. That issue depended on whether he was teaching religion. The defense presented by the school was essentially to the effect that evolution had all the facts and teaching anything but the evolution of man was teaching religion. This was because Darwinism has become so well known in society that it is considered by many to have the answer to everything. Ask an evolutionist how a new animal was created and he'll say that it just happened that certain parts of the DNA molecules connected in a different way and suddenly you may have a wing on a lizard which is a first step in the development of a bird. But a wing on a lizard is much more complicated than such a simple claim. There is entirely different bone pattern in birds. The bones are more like a tube so as to get equal strength with less weight. New joints have to be created, muscles and tendons have to be strengthened. The whole body structure has to be lightened. The digestive system has to be completely changed to eliminate quickly so as to not carry excess weight. Unless all these systems are coordinated a wing is going to be useless and a hindrance such that the animal will not survive."

"There is no limit to what a creative scientist may imagine in his mind. It is so easy to make up imaginary changes that no one can prove or disprove and yet we know that the DNA molecule which creates such complicated animals, contains information, an enormous amount of information. Much more than can be created by a mix up of molecules. Evolutionists cannot explain where this information came from. They try to theorize that all of these things developed gradually but the explosion of new animals in the Cambrian period shows that a great number of new animals popped into existence without a parent to pass on the new characteristics. Without an ancestor there can be no evolution. Darwin himself admitted that. If complex new animals can begin to exist without any possible way for a parent to pass on some new gene, then evolution is entirely wrong?"[7]

"So scientists can't explain how life began. They can't explain how the universe began. Yet they presume to tell us how new species of animals began. They do this even in the face of undisputed evidence that first life began without any known way to explain how or where the immense amount of information necessary to create that animal came from."

"But we know some things for certain. We're talking about first life. We do know that the DNA molecule contains all the information to create protein which is necessary to duplicate cells so life can continue. Since even the first life animal had this information it had to come from somewhere. Remember that Dr. Adler told us that protein is necessary to create DNA and that

DNA is necessary to create protein. One can't occur without the other and there was no ancestor to pass on that information. So that tells me they both came into existence together. That is not a natural occurrence. It's indicative of an intelligent event, a new creature built according to a design or plan to reproduce itself. This indicates intelligent design. And that's not the only indication of intelligent design. Remember the testimony that the universe exploded into existence with logical, orderly principles. Where did these universal rules come from? How did gravity and all of the other universal constants get to be so precisely balanced that life could exist? It's clearly another example of intelligent design."

"So I've illustrated the weakness and fallacies of evolution and the supporting strengths of intelligent design and I'm asking you why should the law be biased to favor evolution and disfavor intelligent design?"

"Evolutionists say that ID is used to promote a belief in God but that is not true. ID proponents only present facts that new complex animal systems need an enormous amount of information to exist. You can make whatever conclusion you want from that knowledge. Evolutionists claim this happens a little at a time over a great amount of time. Of course if this were true it would take millions of years to be passed on from parent to child. We have seen that this was not the case with a great number of first animals in the Cambrian period who exploded into life with no ancestor but their DNA still had the information for cell duplication. Design proponents simply ask, "Where did this information come from?"

"Intelligent design proponents don't say it came from God. They take a true scientific position, they present facts and leave it up to research to determine the answer. But they do take the position that the source of information is intelligence because that is the most logical source based on our knowledge of the rules of the universe. It's so simple it hardly needs telling but for example if you arrive home in the evening and you see a note on the kitchen table which tells you your supper is in the oven you know there is an intelligent agent presenting that information. According to the rules we live by we don't believe that the note just popped into existence by chance or that some chemical attribute of the paper caused the letters to form. That's what the evolutionists are claiming. That's what mindless materialism is, the note just popped into existence, or the chemistry in the paper formed the words. ID proponents choose the most logical cause consistent with our knowledge and experience."

"So it's clear that the difference between evolution and intelligent design is that one attributes the flow of information to intelligence and the other to mindless materialism. Ask yourselves why scientists have such a negative bias to intelligent design? Dr. Hawking and Dr. Boyle among others are well respected because they get published and ID proponents are not respected simply because they are refused publication due to prejudice. The alien seed theory propounded by some is based on the same principles as intelligent design; that an independent agent implanted intelligent information for the design of life. Think about it, they both claim intelligent design. The only difference is that the seed proponents identify it as coming from aliens and the ID proponents leave the cause open to continued research. The only difference between ID and the alien seed theory is that by naming aliens as the cause it eliminates all fear that a deity could be the cause while ID leaves the issue open to any possibility and scientists apparently live in fear of any consideration that there may be a deity."

"Does ID suggest there is a deity? Well they are careful to avoid proclaiming it. If in the future aliens of greatly superior intelligence should reveal themselves and admit they seeded the universe with life it would be perfectly consistent with intelligent design, that is, that the information came from an intelligent agent. Please let us all think logically. There is no logical reason to give consideration to the alien theory or mindless materialism and not intelligent design."

"Please think of what the school board has done in this case. A governmental agency, which is what the school board is, has no right to show favoritism to one theory over another. What If an individual looks at all the facts involved in the creation of life and decides that the whole process is far too complex to have occurred by mere chance. Is it right or fair for the government to prohibit that individual from deciding there must be an intelligent design behind the whole process and considering facts which support that position? What person in government is wise enough to be allowed to make that decision on behalf of a private individual? Is it right that a bureaucrat should make that decision for our society? In our nation we have a jury system that stands as the last bastion of defense against dictatorial bureaucratic mandates. You have the power to prevent such injustice. If you decide that teaching ID is not teaching religion then you can decide that the school board violated the law and that they fired Steve Sylvester wrongly, that they took away his means of making a living, his support for his family. We like to consider the power and authority of our government to be neutral. If it's not neutral and shows a bias as in this case it calls for an award in favor of the plaintiff and I ask you to make Steve Sylvester whole for everything he has suffered, the loss of wages, the humiliation of being fired, the derogation of his abilities in his profession and tagged as a trouble maker. Consider the concern for not having the income to support his family."

"Once again I want to emphasize that we aren't asking you to decide whether or not there is a god. We are not even asking you to decide that intelligent design is a better theory than evolution, although we think it is. But that's not the issue. We are simply asking you to decide that ID has the right to be taught equally with evolution. With that you will be deciding Steve Sylvester was wrongly terminated. I thank you for your patience in listening to the evidence which has been presented in this case and I'm certain you will do your best and render a just and fair decision as you promised Thank you very much"

Chapter Twenty Seven

The jury is now in the jury room, having been given instructions by the judge as to the law. It is a bare room with a long table and chairs done in the same blonde oak as the court room. The jurors are seated at the table and the person chosen by Henry Cobb, Thomas Hale, begins to talk,

"I understand the first thing we're to do is to pick a foreman. I've done this before. It involves keeping track of the votes and keeping everyone following the judge's instructions. I'll volunteer for the position if no one else wants it."

Everyone looks around and seems to have nothing to say. One juror says,

"Go ahead and take the job, no one else seems to want it." Tom responds,

"OK, well the issue the judge instructed us to determine was whether the school board was justified in terminating the plaintiff. The board had a policy of not allowing any religion to be taught in school and so as far as I'm concerned the teacher violated the policy and should be terminated. If everyone agrees with me raise your hand."(Tom puts his hand up).

Another juror, Fred, protests,

"Wait a minute I didn't hear it that way. The judge said we we're to decide if the school board was justified in deciding that the teacher's presentation of facts concerning biology was contrary to scientific principles. That's why Mr. Taylor pointed out that respected scientists believe that information for life could come from a superior intellect other than a deity." Tom retorts,

"You're not going to believe all that metaphysical baloney he's been dropping on us are you? I think that Sylvester guy is trying to pull the wool over our eyes with all his professed ideals. I think he's just out for the money and if any of you fall for his story he's suckered you into his scam."

Tom senses their uncertainty and senses he can overpower them by being aggressive.

"You Judy, are you going to let this money hungry lawyer use his verbal skills to persuade you to give this guy money? I think it's all a scam to take your tax money and put it in his pocket."

Judy shrugs her shoulders and doesn't respond. Fred says,

"Hold on, the judge said we're not supposed to consider the ability to pay or give consideration to any personal interest we think we might have in the case. You're the foreman who's supposed to keep us within the judge's guidelines and here you are violating those guidelines."

"One thing about these jury panels, Fred, is that we're all entitled to voice our opinion. Now I'm trying to build a consensus here and I'm giving my take on the evidence I heard and if you want to have your say go right ahead but I think I can get myself and three others to reach a majority decision here."

"What about you Paul? Do you see my point about this case?"

Paul: responds,

"Well gosh, I kinda thought the lawyer for the teacher made a lot of good points. Particularly with the points point about just letting the kids hear both sides. I don't think the scientists have got such a rock solid case that they should be able to block any other reasonable explanation. But I guess I'm willing to listen to other points of view."

Tom continues his aggressive stance,

"Are you going to let that attorney with his slick way of wording questions and tricking the doctor into saying things he didn't mean, convince you that this intelligent design mumbo jumbo is anything other than an attempt to sell religion to our innocent kids?"

Paul seems timid and doesn't respond. He just lets his head drop.

Fred interjects,

"Look, use some common sense. It is undisputed that first life began without evolution. It's also clear that a great number of new animals just exploded into existence in the Cambrian period without any ancestor. I can't conceive of anyone who would claim that evolution could occur without an ancestor to pass on mutated genes. Let me ask you Tom, are you was willing to say that all this new life began as a result of evolution? If so, can you explain where the evolution came from and what there was to evolve?"

"Those were just one time occurrences, aberrations that no one can explain."

"Aberrations? Have you been listening to the testimony? The defense witness admitted that the information contained in a cell is intelligence and that no one knows where that intelligence for new life came from. Some think it came from alien beings but regardless of where it came from there was new life without evolution. We know it can happen. So who needs evolution? More importantly why does it have such a prominent position in our schools as if it were the only possible answer?"

Fred addresses the other jurors,

"Look people, the defendant's principle witness admitted that intelligent design could be taught as long as there was no claim that God was the designer. The teacher says he's not teaching that and Mr. Taylor pointed out that there is no testimony to prove the teacher was promoting religion. If there was such evidence the attorney for the school board would have emphasized it. It's clear the teacher was wrongfully discharged."

Tom doesn't give up,

"You say it's clear but…"

At this there is a hard knock on the door and Sgt. Ryan enters the room and says,

"Mr. Hale, I'm detective Ryan and you'll have to come with me. You're under arrest for conspiring with Henry Cobb to illegally influence the outcome of a civil trial."

Tom is shocked but never at a loss for words,

"How dare you come into this room and violate the confidentiality of the jury deliberations? Everything that takes place here is confidential. You can't possibly know what I or anyone else has done here so you can't possibly have evidence against me."

"Then you should have been more careful about what you said in your telephone calls Mr. Hale. Are you going to come peacefully? Mr. Cobb is waiting for you in the back seat of my squad car."

Tom shuts up and, his head bowed, goes out with the detective. All on the jury are stunned and speechless.

Chapter Twenty Eight

After the astonishment of seeing the jury foreman taken away under arrest the court re-convenes. There is a legal matter to decide. Since Tom is gone the jury, which is considered one body, no longer exists. It would be improper to proceed with one less juror and either of the attorneys would have a chance to reverse any verdict on appeal if the judge were to proceed with an illegal jury. This would mean that a new trial would be necessary and would double the expense of the case to go through another complete trial. A remedy is possible if both attorneys would agree that they would consent to proceed with the remaining jury.

The judge is on the bench. There is a new clerk who replaces Henry. The court reporter is present as are both attorneys, Judge DeLato speaks to the two attorneys who stand before him,

"Gentlemen you've now been advised that Mr. Cobb has apparently devised a scheme to put a person on the jury who would aggressively argue for a predetermined verdict. Mr. Taylor it was during your Bigg's trial that this first occurred as far as we know. It turns out that one of the jurors in that case finally called the reporter who covered the trial and complained about the influence exercised by the jury foreman. He claimed that the jury in that case was bullied into a verdict that they really didn't want. The reporter noticed that my clerk seemed to be good friends with some powerful people. We don't know who those powerful people are yet but we'll find out."

"Mr. Cobb had a lot of expensive items that didn't seem compatible with a clerk's salary. The reporter went to the police and they developed the evidence to charge the parties. The foreman in the Bigg's case has agreed to testify so it's clear that case was corrupted and I assume you will make a motion for a retrial in that case Mr. Taylor. But in the instant case you have the option of a mistrial or in lieu of a retrial I think you can waive that and proceed with one less juror. If you do you will have waived any appeal you may have on that issue. What do you want to do counsel?"

Creighton answers,

"On behalf of my client your honor we are willing to proceed with the remaining jurors in order to avoid the unnecessary expense of another trial."

John concurs,

"We agree also you honor"

"Very well then, you both agree to waive any objection to continuing this trial. I'll call the jury back into court and instruct them as to what's taken place and that they are to continue to deliberate based on the evidence they have heard without giving any consideration to the juror who's been dismissed because he had an economic interest in the outcome of the case"

Both attorneys say,

"Thank you your honor."

Chapter Twenty Nine

The jury has resumed its deliberation in the jury room. The court room is empty except for John, Pam, Danny and Steve who are waiting for the verdict .To Pam the waiting is torture. She asks,

"They've been deliberating for four hours now and we have no word. Do you think the judge will keep them beyond dinner time?"

John replies,

"We'll just have to wait. This is always the hardest part of the trial when I sit here and think of all the things I should have done and wish I had."

"John you were brilliant. Your cross exam brought out everything you wanted. How you were able to get all the testimony from Dr. Adler which actually helped your case I'll never know. It couldn't have gone any better."

"I can give credit to Steve for educating me and Danny and you for your research but I hope I didn't get into too much detail so that I confused everybody. Throughout the trial I lived in fear that the jury wouldn't be able to follow along. This type of mental exercise is foreign to most people. No I shouldn't say that. It's not foreign to them because everyone uses good common sense. It's just that most of us don't get into thinking about how things began. We have enough trouble dealing with things as they are."

The judge enters the court room along with the new clerk and the court reporter. Judge DeLato announces,

"I've called opposing counsel Mr. Taylor. It seems the jury has reached a verdict."

Creighton comes in.

"Well John, now we'll see if you were able to convince the jury to believe in ghosts. The way I see it the whole thing is preposterous."

"I assume you're referring to believing in alien universes Creighton."

The jury comes in and is seated. It is common for the attorneys and the parties to stand when the jury comes in and for all parties in the court room to stand when the judge takes the bench. Judge DeLato sits down and asks,

"Members of the jury have you reached a verdict?"

This is a civil case with only 6 jurors required and with Thomas Hale gone there are now five.

The Foreman is now Fred.

"We have your honor."

By this time the word has reached the media and several reporters enter the court room and are seated. The new clerk takes the paper from the foreman and gives it to the judge. The judge reads it and hands it to the clerk who reads,

"We the jury find in answer to the special question that intelligent design is an equally valid concept as evolution and that it was wrongful to terminate Stephen Sylvester. As to the second question we find damages in favor of the plaintiff in the amount of $1,000,000."

There is murmuring among the press and excitement all around. Some reporters rush out talking on their cell phones. Pam jumps up and hugs John who is standing. He holds the hug for a moment obviously enjoying it. Steve shakes his hand, congratulating John.

The judge thanks the jury for their efforts and dismisses them. John nods a "Thank you" to the jury as they file out.

A remaining reporter asks,

"Mr. Taylor how does it feel to have proven there is a God? This is going to make national news. I can see the headlines: 'The second Scopes monkey trial allows religion to be taught in schools.'"

John scolds the reporter,

"You know all along I've been saying that's not what the case was about."

"Maybe so but our version makes better press. What does this do to the separation of church and state provision of the constitution counsel? "

"Separation of church and state is not a phrase in the constitution. The prohibition in the constitution is that congress shall not establish a religion. Nor shall congress interfere with the free exercise thereof. The media have educated people to the first part of that phrase and ignored the latter part. Why don't you put that part in your newspaper and feature accuracy instead of sensationalism?"

Pam interjects,

"That's enough questions for now. We've got some business to attend to."

Chapter Thirty

The events the parties have been through, the tension of the trial, the revelation of the attempt to influence the jury, the arrest of the initial jury foreman, then the tension of waiting in the court room and the final explosive impact of the verdict has been exhausting. Back in John's office now are John, Pam, Frank, Katy and Danny. They're watching a TV interview of John on the evening news program. The host is saying that John has made a surprising case for intelligent design and asking how he got into that field of physics. John replies,

"Once I got into it there was no magic involved. It was just a matter of common sense and keeping an open mind. It's not beyond understanding of the average person. It's just that people don't usually take the time to consider such matters as they face every day problems in their lives and that's too bad. People should have an idea of where they stand in the grand scheme of things, where they come from, where they're going, and what is their purpose in life. Whether that purpose is to simply fulfill the design of an alien seed or to worship God."

The host asks if John is a religious person. He replies,

"Yes I am and more so after my preparation for this case got me to thinking. I found a verse in Romans 1:19&20 that says that God's power has been shown to man in the things that have been made. Paul's talking about the earth and the stars that testify to an infinite power who can create such a wonderful universe and that this should be obvious to man so that they have no excuse."

"Paul goes on to say that some, claiming to be wise, become fools. That, to me, seemed to tie in pretty much with the current thinking of renowned academicians who close their minds to design which seems so obvious to a reasonable person. It seemed to me that the way the trial developed fell right in line with what Paul said about 20 centuries ago."

The host looks at the camera and says "Well there you are folks. John Taylor has convinced a jury that the universe and the life that exists on this earth was the product of design. He says you can easily figure it out if you keep an open mind. And that it's perhaps the most important decision you might make in your life. 'Thank you for coming Mr. Taylor'."

John thanks the host and the segment ends. Frank says,

"I've got to hand it to you John. In your cross exam of Dr. Adler you made it clear that no matter how pompous and assertive the elitists are, there are important factors that are either unknown, uncertain or unanswered which preclude the dogmatic statements propounded by those who claim to know it all."

"You give me too much credit Frank. The information I used to cross examine Dr. Adler was provided by Steve and my sterling staff of Pam and Danny."

Pam disagrees,

"John, we may have given you some facts but there's a knack to the way the questions are asked and the timing of it all; the pauses, the glance at the jury when you've made a point. Those are the skills of a masterful trial attorney and you mastered them perfectly. That's been acknowledged throughout the legal community. You're a rising star as a trial lawyer and that's why you got a job offer from Brooks, King and Goodwin, one of the most prestigious trial firms in the country."

Frank says, it doesn't get any better than that firm, John. What are you going to do?"

"There was a time Frank when that was what I wanted most in life. But I've changed. I know what that type of practice entails in those high pressure firms. You spend weeks away from home on cases all over the United States. You refuse reasonable settlement offers in order to push for big jury verdicts to keep the firm's name in the headlines. Lose a case and everything you've done in the past is forgotten. It's living in a pressure cooker. I've learned from Steve Sylvester that doing what's right for you is more important than prestige. Steve settled the case for my attorney fee and his lost wages in return for returning to his job. He's doing what he feels is right. He never wanted anything more than that. I want that kind of life. Besides as he puts his arm around Pam, I've got some interests in staying close to home with someone that's become an important part of my life. Pam and John smile at each other as Frank and the others look on approvingly."

Frank asks,

"Are you two about to make an announcement about an upcoming event?"

John answers,

"Just as soon as the details are worked out."

He hugs Pam who welcomes his embrace as the others join in congratulating the couple when, surprisingly, the president/ leader of the school board walks into the office.

The leader, seeming somewhat embarrassed says,

"Sorry, am I interrupting something?"

John, not sure of whether this was an apologetic or an accusatory visit says,

"That's alright sir. How can I help you?"

"I wanted to thank you for settling for a reduced amount. It helps us to balance the budget for the coming year. But there's another problem. We will keep our promise to return Steve to his teaching position. However I've just been advised that the Woman's Alliance for Justice has filed a suit in federal court alleging a constitutional violation for teaching religion. The board has decided that you are the best one to defend the school in this coming suit, if you are willing to accept."

Frank comments,

"It looks like you've carved out a specialty for yourself in the legal field counsel."

"Maybe so Frank but it sounds like the right thing to do."

John shakes the leader's hand as he smiles at Pam.

Copyright 2013 Vance Cartright —The issues in this story are dramatized so as to represent the strong feelings of persons involved with this issue. It further is intended to emphasize the importance of questioning the manner of the government's interference in an area in which they have no right to dictate close questions involving important beliefs. In addition it is intended to emphasize the importance of making the right choice in how the education system influences our students. The characters portrayed herein are fictional and not intended to depict any real person or persons.

End Notes

1. See "the Design of Life", Demski/Wells, The Foundation for Thought and Ethics, 2008, p253, quoting Collins "no serious scientist would currently claim that a naturalistic explanation for the origin of life is at hand."
2. House of Cards, Tom Bethel, Discovery Institute, page 182
3. Darwin's Doubt, Stephen Meyers, Harper One, page 70
4. Beginning and End, Isaac Asimov, 1977
5. Signs of Intelligence, Baker Book House, page 160, 2001
6. Panspermia, see Wikipedia
7. Darwin's Doubt, Stephen Meyer, Harper One, pages 17-23

Made in the USA
Middletown, DE
31 January 2019